I0817344

EYE ON ART

Anime

Japanese Animation Comes to America

By Kenneth Bartolotta

Portions of this book originally appeared in *Anime* by Hal Marcovitz.

LUCENT PRESS

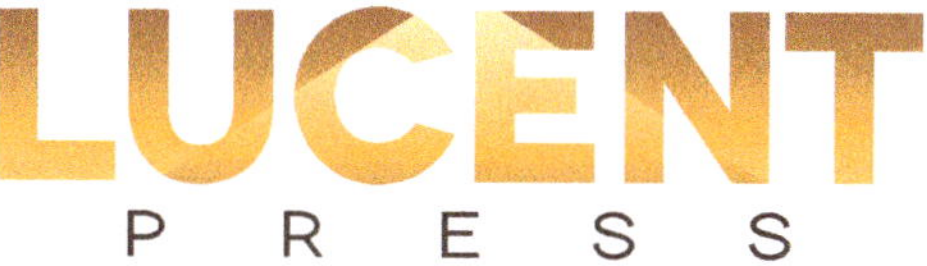

Published in 2018 by
Lucent Press, an Imprint of Greenhaven Publishing, LLC
353 3rd Avenue
Suite 255
New York, NY 10010

Designer: Seth Hughes
Editor: Jennifer Lombardo

Cataloging-in-Publication Data

Names: Bartolotta, Kenneth.
Title: Anime: Japanese animation comes to America / Kenneth Bartolotta.
Description: New York : Lucent Press, 2018. | Series: Eye on art | Includes index.
Identifiers: ISBN 9781534561021 (library bound) | ISBN 9781534561038 (ebook)
Subjects: LCSH: Animated films–Japan–Juvenile literature.
Classification: LCC NC1766.J3 M28 2018 | DDC 791.43'340952–dc23

Printed in the United States of America

CPSIA compliance information: Batch #BS17KL: For further information contact Greenhaven Publishing LLC, New York, New York at 1-844-317-7404.

Please visit our website, www.greenhavenpublishing.com. For a free color catalog of all our high-quality books, call toll free 1-844-317-7404 or fax 1-844-317-7405.

Contents

Foreword

When many people think of art, the first things that come to mind may be paintings, drawings, sculptures, or even pictures created entirely with a computer. However, people have been applying artistic elements to almost every aspect of life for thousands of years. Human beings love beautiful things, and they seek beauty in unlikely places. Buildings, clothes, furniture, and many other things we use every day can all have an artistic aspect to them.

Attempts to define art have frequently fallen short. Merriam-Webster defines art as "something that is created with imagination and skill and that is beautiful or that expresses important ideas or feelings." However, almost no one refers to the dictionary definition when attempting to decide whether or not something can be considered art. They rely on their intuition, which leaves much room for debate between competing opinions. What one person views as beautiful, another may see as ugly. An idea that an artist feels it is important to express may hit home with some people and be dismissed by others. Some people believe that art should always be beautiful, while others feel that art should be unsettling enough to pull people out of their comfort zone. With all of these contradictory views, it is no wonder that the question of what is art is so often disputed.

This series aims to introduce readers to some of the more unconventional and controversial art forms, such as anime, fashion design, and graffiti. Debate on these topics has often been heated, with some people firmly declaring that they are art and others declaring just as firmly that they are not. Each book in the series discusses the history of a particular art form, the ways it is created, and the reasons why it is considered artistic. Learning more about these topics helps young adults recognize the art that is all around them as well as form their own opinions about this complex subject.

Quotes by experts in various art fields enhance the engaging text. All quotes are cited so readers can trace them back to their original source, giving them a starting point for further research. A list of recommended books and websites also allows young adults to delve deeper into related subjects. Full-color photographs give vivid examples of the artistic works being described in the books so readers can visualize the terms they are learning.

Through this series, young adults gain a better understanding of a variety of popular art forms. They also develop a deeper appreciation for the artistry that is inherent in the things they see and use every day.

INTRODUCTION

Anime: A Global Phenomenon

The world of anime has become a global phenomenon. Its reach extends well beyond the country of Japan from which it originated. Anime (pronounced AA-nuh-may) is Japanese animation which has found vast audiences in America as well as other countries across the globe. In the United States, anime refers only to Japanese animation, but in Japan, the word refers to all styles of animation, including Western animation. For the purposes of this book, the term "anime" will refer to Japanese animation only. In Japan, anime earns more than $5 billion per year. From broadcast and cable TV to movie theaters and home viewing, anime is enjoyed in all sorts of viewing formats. In addition to viewing anime, fans may also find the same stories and more in print as manga (pronounced MON-gah).

Anime is an art form that represents a number of distinct styles. Though most widely known for its iconic large eyes and vibrant colors, character design and proportions vary based on the artist's particular style. Themes likewise range from tragedy to comedy; happy endings are never guaranteed.

Doraemon, one of the most ubiquitous manga and anime characters in Japan, is written and illustrated by Fujiko F. Fujio, the pen name of artists Hiroshi Fujimoto and Motoo Abiko. Originally published in 1969, Doraemon is a household name for children and adults alike.

The World of Anime

Anime has been produced in Japan for nearly a century, and manga's origins go back even further; many people believe the first manga were created in the 12th and 13th centuries, although the word "manga" was not used until 1798. Manga is the genre of graphic novels and comic books that sometimes, but not always, tell the same stories on the printed page that anime tells on the screen. Early anime was often based on characters and stories that initially appeared in manga. Even today, much of anime is adapted from manga, just as many American films are adapted from comic books, novels and similar sources.

The anime that most Americans see in theaters or on TV is a fraction of what is produced in Japan. Most of the anime available in America features adventure or science fiction stories, but in Japan, anime is used by filmmakers and TV show directors to tell a variety of stories, including romances, mysteries, historical dramas, sports dramas, slapstick comedies, and fairy tales. Writer Shinobu Price said, "The only thing that really classifies anime as, well, anime is the fact that it is made in Japan by Japanese artists within a Japanese context. Stylistic experimentation with the medium is expected—rewarded if it's good … The creative realm of anime is vast, the possibilities endless."[1]

In America, anime was regarded for years as an art form appreciated mostly by teenagers—although there are exceptions, such as the Pokémon video games, films, and TV shows that appeal to young children. This may be because in Western culture, comics and cartoons have historically been considered to be for children and young adults. However, over the years, American adults began realizing that the stories told in anime and manga were deep and complex, and many came to appreciate the art form. This has long been the case in Japan; there, audiences range from very young children to adults.

In America, manga can be found on the shelves of most bookstores. Many libraries that have created graphic novel sections are sure to include manga titles among the selections. As with anime, though, manga is far more widespread in Japan than in America. Though recent years have seen a decline in both overall book and manga sales in Japan, recent market reports have shown jumps in manga sales. This has been credited to fan devotion to particular series with anime or live-action adaptations, such as *Attack on Titan* and *One Piece*.

Some Americans grew up watching anime without realizing it. In the 1960s, the first Japanese anime stories started appearing on American TV with the broadcasts of such shows

©Tezuka Productions

KYOTO
手塚治虫ワールド

Some Americans believe all anime looks the same, but this poster shows the wide range of styles anime artists use for their characters.

as *Astro Boy*, *Kimba the White Lion*, and *Speed Racer*. The TV shows were dubbed into English—in other words, the lines of dialogue were re-recorded in English and synced up to the action—and edited so that most of the Japanese content was taken out. For example, a scene in which the characters dine with chopsticks would typically be cut out of the American version. Generally, the only hint that the shows originated in Japan came at the end when the credits rolled by, giving the young viewers reason to wonder why all the creative people involved in the production of the shows seemed to have Japanese names.

Anime Comes to America

Beginning in the late 1970s, the anime explosion hit American pop culture. Due to the huge popularity of anime in Japan and the increasing ease of exchanging cultural elements between different countries, American distributors began importing it to the United States. They started with only a few titles, but soon video rental stores featured entire anime shelves. The appeal of anime initially spread through word of mouth; people fell deeply in love with it, and the first U.S. anime fan club was created in 1977. It did not take long after that for American studios, TV networks, and publishers to get the message about anime and manga, and their popularity exploded. A large part of this success was due to continuing marketing campaigns; originally, anime was marketed only for children, and toys based on the anime characters were in high demand.

As for what was going on up there on the screen, Americans who were used to seeing the animation produced by the Walt Disney animation studio for such films as *The Little Mermaid* and *Aladdin* saw far different stories unfold in Japanese anime. In the Disney films, young heroes and heroines overcome great odds to defeat the villains, find love, and live happily ever after. In Japanese anime, the stories are often far darker, the motives of the heroes are not always righteous, the villains are often misunderstood, and seldom does anybody seem to live happily ever after. This sometimes caused problems when they were adapted for an audience of Western children; characters that died were often described as "only resting." According to some experts, these types of characteristics found in anime stories are largely responsible for attracting a huge adult audience to the genre. Dr. Nissim Otmazgin, chair of the Department of Asian Studies at the Hebrew University of Jerusalem, wrote,

According to anime specialist Roland Kelts, young Americans were looking for new excite-

Anime artists drew inspiration from Disney and other Western animation but kept their own unique style. For instance, just as both of Mickey Mouse's ears are visible no matter which way he turns his head, both of Astro Boy's hair spikes are always visible.

ment and cultural products. This reflects a sense of fatigue in homegrown productions with the same old narratives being used repeatedly. In this respect, anime came at a time when the American market needed "new blood," according to him. In the 1990s, the American industry was just not able to produce enough exciting productions and it was at this point that anime arrived with its fascinating repertoire of evolving narratives and a new set of images (even though anime had already been introduced on television).[2]

With smaller budgets with which to work, Japanese animators often produced a rougher and more static form of animated art than Western studios, such as Disney. However, many people enjoy the distinctive drawing style, and the appeal of the stories cannot be denied. Additionally, from the 1960s onward, many Western studios used Japanese studios to complete their animation, so Western viewers became more familiar with the art style. These factors have helped manga as well as anime capture a truly dedicated audience of fans in America.

CHAPTER ONE

Anime's Origins

From the 12th century onward, Japan has enjoyed a long history of rich storytelling through pictures. The tradition began when *Tale of Genji*, a national epic, was illustrated by artists nearly 100 years after it was written. Considered to be history's first novel, *Tale of Genji* was written by Murasaki Shikibu, a lady-in-waiting to the Japanese empress Akiko. Still in publication 1,000 years after it was written, *Tale of Genji* features the heroic and romantic adventures of Genji, the warrior prince.

Originally read as one long, unrolling scroll, the 54-chapter story was illustrated in a format known as *emakimono*. *Emakimono* is an illustrated scroll that combines both words and pictures, all of which are laid out horizontally. In Japan, words are laid out and read from right to left instead of left to right.

Besides *emakimono*, artists were also dabbling in other art forms. One such art form was *giga*, which in English, translates to "funny pictures." Unlike *emakimono* style, *giga* featured much shorter and more compact stories.

Giga and *emakimono* are generally considered to be the beginnings of anime and manga, although some scholars believe works from as early as the 8th century may have had an influence on the art form. Many sources also link modern manga to a series of sketches created by Japanese artist Katsushika Hokusai in the early 19th century.

While both manga and anime are forms of art that originated in Japan, they are sometimes adapted for Western audiences. Fans often debate these changes and have strong opinions about them.

Tale of Genji is an example of emakimono. It is one of Japan's most important works of literature and is considered to be groundbreaking in terms of telling stories through pictures.

Japan Punch and *Tobae*

In the 1860s, two Europeans arrived in Japan and soon became influential figures in the development of Japanese comic art. Charles Wirgman, a British journalist, established a publication he titled *Japan Punch*, which was styled after the British version of the magazine that had been published in London for around 20 years. *Japan Punch* featured comic strips, which the Japanese called *ponchi*, a word based on the title of the publication. Meanwhile, a competing publication, *Tobae*, was established by George Bigot, a French painter living in Japan. The title of the publication was drawn from the name of 12th-century *emakimono* artist Sojo Toba. Many Japanese artists drew inspiration from these publications, and some started their own magazines.

Western Influence

By the 19th century, Europeans and Americans had started making their way to Japan. Trade between Japan and the Western world commenced, particularly after Commodore Matthew Perry signed a treaty with Japan in 1854, establishing diplomatic relations between the United States and the Asian nation. The Japanese soon became dedicated readers of newspapers and magazines published in Europe and America that arrived aboard ships docking in Tokyo and other cities. Japanese readers were particularly fond of *Punch* and *Puck*, satirical British magazines that told most of their stories in cartoons.

By the late 1800s, Japanese versions of *Punch* and *Puck*, as well as many other magazines of cartoon art, had been established in Tokyo and other Japanese cities. Among the top artists of the era were Ippei Okamoto and Rakuten Kitazawa. Born in 1876, Kitazawa became a newspaper cartoonist in Japan; his most popular cartoon told of the ongoing comic antics of Donsha, a street orphan. He also helped found *Tokyo Puck*, the Japanese version of the British magazine.

Okamoto, who was born in 1886, helped organize Japanese comic artists into a professional association known as Nippon Mangakai. Okamoto was well traveled. He visited the United States shortly after alcohol was banned by Prohibition and reported back to his countrymen that Americans had found comfort in the Sunday comics. He wrote, "The American people love to laugh, but not in the stiff manner of the British. Their laugh is an innocent one that instantly dispels fatigue … American comics have become an entertainment equal to baseball, motion pictures and the presidential elections. Some observers say that comics have replaced alcohol as a solace for workers since Prohibition began."[3]

Meanwhile, artists were working in other mediums. In 1917, a 19-year-old amateur filmmaker named Oten Shimokawa, a former editorial assistant at *Tokyo Puck*, produced a five-minute animated cartoon called *Imokawa Mukuzo Genkanban no Maki*. (In English, this translates to *Mukuzo Imokawa, the Doorman*.) It is regarded as the first anime film. That same year, another animator, Junichi Kouchi, produced a two-minute cartoon about a samurai who is tricked into buying a dull sword. The following year, Seitaro Kitayama created a movie about a fisherman who is brought by a giant turtle to an underwater world. Kouchi and Kitayama have been called the "fathers of Japanese anime;"[4] their short films provided inspiration for future generations of anime filmmakers.

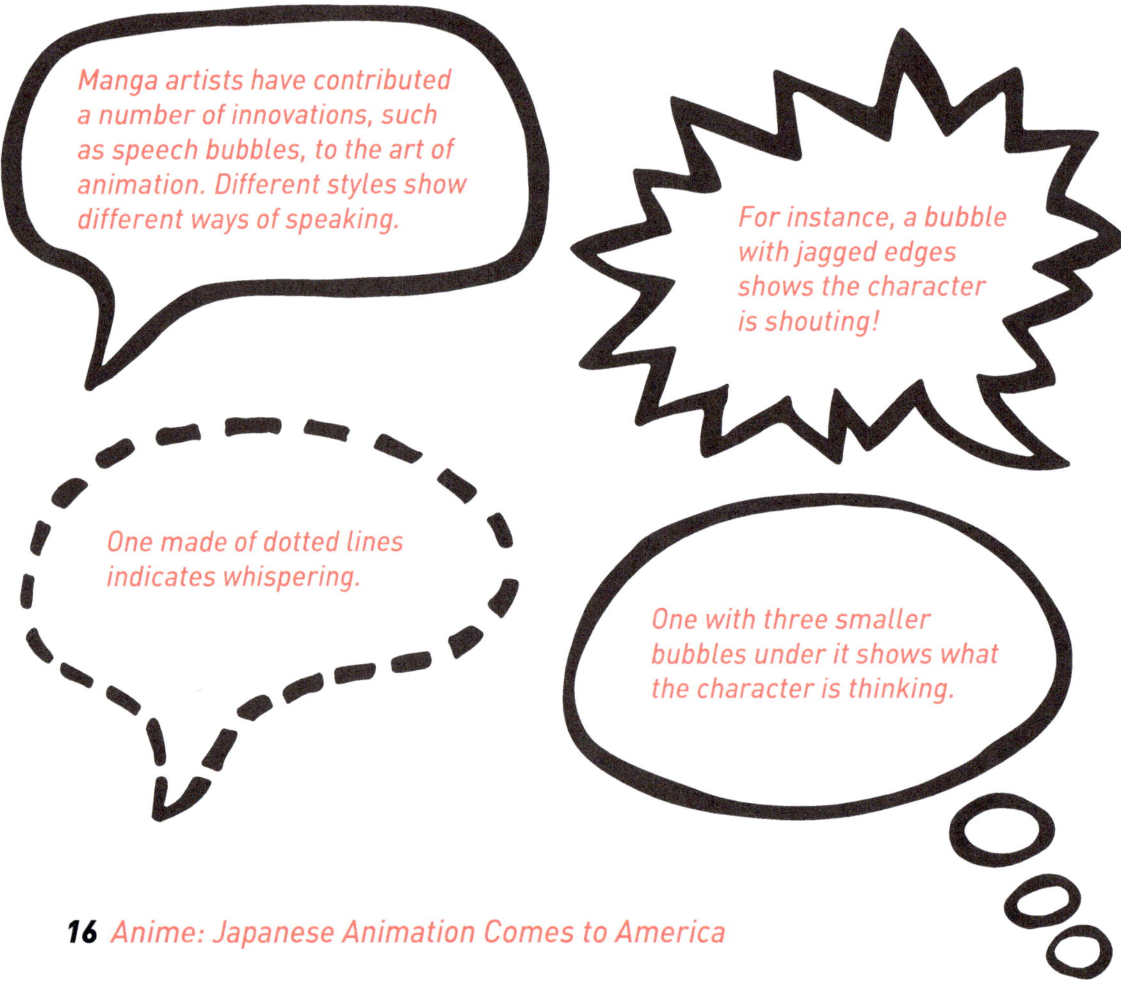

Anime During Times of War

The images drawn by the early animators were crude by today's standards, and over the next few years, Japanese animators experimented with a number of different processes to make their pictures move on the screen. In 1928, when Walt Disney unveiled *Steamboat Willie*, showing a crisply drawn Mickey Mouse navigating over a choppy river, Japanese artists were experimenting with animating characters they cut out of paper. Animators used the medium to tell stories that were fun to watch about animals causing mischief and plucky children outwitting oafish adults. Japanese folktales were also brought to life in these early examples of anime.

That changed by the 1930s, when a military regime took control of the country. As Japan prepared for war, the government encouraged animators to portray the adventures of heroes performing deeds to save the nation from foreign aggressors. In 1931, a folk hero named Momotaro was shown leading the Japanese navy into battle against all manner of cartoon villains. Momotaro and the navy always won. In one anime film, produced in 1933 and titled *Black Cat Banzai*, Momotaro repels an invasion of bombers flown by an army of rodents who closely resemble Mickey Mouse. After Japan invaded China in 1937, all films, including anime, had to be approved by government censors. Only those films containing a strong message of propaganda and designed to lift the spirits of the population were approved.

Following the Japanese attack on Pearl Harbor in 1941, the regime stepped up calls for propaganda films, but Japanese animators were disadvantaged by the war economy. By that time, Japanese animators were making films the same way animators made them elsewhere: The images were drawn on translucent cels, which were placed against a nonmoving background and photographed cel by cel with movie film. The cels were made out of cellulose, which is the substance that gives plants their structure. However, cellulose is a key ingredient in weapons making, and that is what most of Japan's cellulose supply was used for during the war. As a result, much of the anime produced during World War II has been destroyed. To save cels, animators would use the cellulose sheets, then wash off the images so they could be reinked. Still, a lot of anime was produced during the war, and much of it was made with money provided by the military. Many anime films featured Momotaro, who was still protecting Japan from invaders.

As the war dragged on and it became increasingly clear to Japanese leaders that they were going to lose, they stepped up calls for animation to prop up the spirits of the people.

In the tale of Momotaro, a young boy protects Japan from evil. In Momotaro's Divine Sea Warriors, *he leads an army of animals such as the two shown here.*

In April 1945, at a time when the Japanese Imperial Navy was otherwise preoccupied with preparing for an anticipated Allied invasion of the island, its admirals still found the resources to finance one last Momotaro adventure. The film, titled *Momotaro's Divine Sea Warriors*, was the first feature-length anime movie produced in Japan. The film shows Momotaro leading a band of monkeys, rabbits, and other cute critters into an air strike that conquers a British fort in the Pacific. The film ends with children pretending to parachute onto a chalk outline of North America, with the last child stomping on it upon landing.

The Story of Momotaro

The character of Momotaro comes from a Japanese fairy tale. In the story, an elderly couple is sad because they have no children. One day, the woman is washing clothes in the river when she sees a giant peach floating in the water. She takes the peach home so she and her husband can eat it for dinner, but when she goes to cut it open, a voice from inside tells her not to cut the peach. Suddenly, the peach splits open, and a young boy jumps out.

The couple is overjoyed to finally have a son, and they name him Momotaro, which means "Peach Boy." When he is 15 years old, Momotaro tells his parents it his duty to protect Japan from the evil ogres that often come from the sea to steal from the Japanese and murder them. With an army made up of a dog, a monkey, and a type of bird called a pheasant, Momotaro goes to the island of the ogres, defeats them, steals their treasure, and returns home victorious. Because Momotaro is a protector of Japan, it made sense for animators to make propaganda films about him during World War II.

Osamu Tezuka: A True Visionary

After Japan's defeat in 1945, the animation and publishing industries—as with most of the rest of the Japanese economy—were in shambles. At the end of the war, the Americans and British arrived to install a democratic government, rebuild Japanese infrastructure and industry, and find jobs for millions of unemployed workers. Reestablishing the anime and manga industries was not a top priority for the officials in charge of Japanese reconstruction. For the first few years following the war, few theaters were in operation, and they showed mostly American and British films made available to audiences by the occupying armies. Essentially, there was no new anime produced and hardly any manga available. Rarely could readers afford to buy manga anyway, so something of a "manga rental" industry grew up after the war. Instead of selling the books, bookstores rented the titles to readers. Author and anime expert Gilles Poitras said,

> *The decade after the war was a hard one for both anime and cinema due to the great damage inflicted upon the country. Many theaters and production venues had been destroyed. All the same, the manga industry grew as a cheap form of entertainment that did not require buildings and projectors; one could easily rent manga from special shops, predecessors to video stores.*[5]

Indeed, out of the rubble of World War II grew the foundations of today's anime and manga industries, and it was due mostly to the efforts of a single artist. Osamu Tezuka is often referred to as the "Walt Disney of Japan." Just as Disney helped launch the animation industry in the United States, Tezuka is given credit as the most influential anime and manga artist in Japan.

Born in 1928, Tezuka entered medical school shortly after World War II. He obtained a medical degree, but by then, he was already a busy manga artist. He soon dropped his medical career to concentrate on manga. As the publishing industry slowly recovered from the war, publishers needed qualified artists to produce manga titles. Tezuka soon became a busy artist, providing illustrations for a number of Japanese publications, including children's picture books, adventure stories for teens, and detective stories for adults. In 1947, Tezuka wrote and illustrated a 200-page graphic novel titled *New Treasure Island*, which is regarded as the first modern work of manga. Japanese readers embraced the title, buying around

400,000 copies. In producing *New Treasure Island* and other titles, Tezuka essentially used animation or cinematic techniques to tell a story in a printed format. He changed viewpoints often—for instance, in one frame, he might show a character from afar and in the next, illustrate the character in an extreme close-up. Tezuka also developed the technique still employed today by manga and anime artists of using his characters' facial expressions as much as dialogue to tell the story. American author and anime authority Frederik L. Schodt said,

> *Tezuka was a real pioneer. He was trying to use the comic book medium to tell stories. He was one of the first people who seriously tried to use manga in this way, just as film directors use film or novelists use novels. As a result, his stories are very thought-provoking. There's always something that children can enjoy, but actually adults can enjoy them too because they have many layers of meaning. There is a superficial layer which is just entertainment, but there is often a very philosophical layer, just like in a good movie or novel.*[6]

Manga Cafés, Libraries, and Museums

Manga is so popular in Japan that entrepreneurs have established manga cafés and manga libraries. These are places where fans can read manga while they eat, drink coffee, and discuss the latest titles with other readers. There are hundreds of manga cafés and libraries in Tokyo alone.

Some manga cafés stock as many as 30,000 titles on their shelves. At a manga café, customers order food or coffee and relax while they read through the latest manga titles. A manga library is not like the typical public library found in America. Since the manga libraries do not sell food or drinks, customers are charged an hourly fee to read the manga on the libraries' shelves. Library customers are free to bring their own food and beverages, though.

Manga cafés and libraries are found in most Japanese cities. Some cities have also established museums dedicated to popular manga artists and their work. Saitma Manga Kaikan, located in an area of the city of Saitama called Omiya, was Japan's first manga museum. It has a permanent exhibition on Rakuten Kitazawa. The city of Takarazuka, where Osamu Tezuka lived as a boy, has created a museum dedicated to the work of the pioneering manga and anime artist. Additionally, the Ghibli Museum, dedicated to anime produced by the famous Studio Ghibli, is so popular that advance reservations are required.

There are many places in Tokyo where customers can eat and drink while reading rented manga. Additionally, several manga and anime museums have been established, such as the Osamu Tezuka Manga Museum (shown below) in Takarazuka, the Japanese city where Tezuka grew up.

Astro Boy

During the 1950s, Tezuka expanded manga into many genres, finding audiences from very young children to adults. In Japan, the first readers of manga were teenagers. As they grew older, Tezuka developed titles in romance, mystery, drama, and other adult-oriented fiction to keep them reading manga as adults. He was well known for challenging the idea that manga and anime themes should be exclusively juvenile, but he also produced manga for young children, generally featuring cute and magical animal characters in fairy tale–style adventures. Before he turned his attention to developing anime in the early 1960s, Tezuka produced a stunning amount of manga. It is believed he wrote and illustrated more than 700 volumes of manga that included around 170,000 pages.

Meanwhile, during the 1950s, independent animators found a way to restart the industry that had virtually disappeared after Momotaro's last adventure at the end of the war. Like Tezuka, the Japanese artists working in anime were strongly influenced by the films of the Disney studio, and they concentrated on stories featuring old Japanese folk tales. In 1960, Tezuka agreed to permit a group of independent artists to animate one of his manga stories, *Alakazam the Great*. The manga book and its subsequent film told the story of a young monkey king who challenges the gods and is then sent back to Earth to learn humility and serve as the bodyguard for a prince. Tezuka quickly realized the potential of the new genre and believed that Japanese audiences would welcome fast-paced adventure stories featuring heroic characters. With television growing as a medium of entertainment in Japan, Tezuka decided to concentrate on producing content for Japanese TV rather than theatrical release. In 1961, he created Japan's first animation studio, called Mushi Productions, which is still active today. Mushi's first show was titled *Tetsuwan Atom*—in English, *Mighty Atom*—which was based on one of Tezuka's manga titles from 1953. The show told the story of a robot boy created by a grieving scientist as a replacement for his dead son. It was, in a way, a science fiction retelling of *Pinocchio*.

Along with the action as well as its good-versus-evil scenario, Tezuka ensured that *Tetsuwan Atom* would include strong characters who showed human emotions and concerns. Tezuka found that he could constantly refine the characters as the story progressed from week to week. Of course, there was a strong dose of science fiction served up to the viewers as well: Atom, a true superhero, could speak 60 languages and fly by converting his feet into

Osamu Tezuka is shown here on a postage stamp with four of his most famous characters. In order from top to bottom, they are Black Jack, Princess Knight, Kimba the White Lion, and Astro Boy.

jet engines. He also possessed super strength, super vision, and super hearing and could shoot lasers out of his hips. His heart could detect people's evil intentions. In creating this character, Tezuka was inspired by both Superman and Pinocchio. Eventually, Tezuka provided Atom with a robot sister and an evil twin brother. *Tetsuwan Atom* soon became enormously popular in Japan. Each week, an estimated 40 percent of all households in Japan tuned in to watch the robot boy's next adventure. If Tezuka was the Walt Disney of Japan, then Mighty Atom was his Mickey Mouse. American anime authority Fred Patten wrote,

> *It was an instant success, completely transforming animation in Japan, by showing there was a vast public demand for comic book–style action-adventure in modern or futuristic settings. It also showed that the public would accept TV-quality animation; limited but fast-paced. This effectively put the individual artist-animators out of business, since they could not produce cartoons fast enough for the TV market, but enabled several fledgling animators to get the financial backing to start their own studios.*[7]

Tetsuwan Atom premiered on Japanese TV in 1963 and remained a staple of Japanese anime for three years. Nearly 200 episodes were aired. A few months after its debut on Japanese TV, an American TV producer imported the series, had it dubbed into English, and changed the name to *Astro Boy*. Japanese anime had now arrived in America.

Americanizing Anime

While *Astro Boy* was America's first exposure to anime, the production and artwork of the show was not considered revolutionary. Heavily edited to fit into an American TV format, the show was confusing to viewers. In addition, the show's animation was not the same as more established American cartoons such as *The Flintstones*, *Bugs Bunny*, *The Bullwinkle Show*, and *Huckleberry Hound*.

However, regardless of its technical shortcomings, many considered *Astro Boy* a pioneer in the field of animation. The show's debut was followed by an influx of Japanese animation in America. Shows from Japan found audiences in the United States, and in the coming years, both the quality and the content of Japanese-produced shows improved.

The influx of shows led to a devoted following among Americans who were starved for stories featuring science fiction, adventure, and fantasy. In the catalogue of past Japanese shows, fans found a new form of entertainment. Much of this popularity was attributed to the debut of *Astro Boy*. As Patten stated, "*Astro Boy* proved that a Japanese animated series could be successful in North America, paving the way for all that followed."[8]

Astro Boy is considered America's first exposure to Japanese animation. The character is still widely popular today.

Producing a Pilot

When *Tetsuwan Atom* premiered on Japanese TV, it was inked and broadcast in black and white because Tezuka's studio did not have the budget to produce a color cartoon, nor did the Fuji Television Network own the equipment to broadcast in color. In the early 1960s, there were few color TVs in Japan anyway, although they were far more common by 1964.

When an NBC television network executive who was based in Japan turned on his TV and saw an episode featuring the exploits of the brave little rocket boy, he thought it might have potential in America. The executive obtained some copies of the show from Fuji and shipped them back to NBC in New York. After receiving the copies, the network got in touch with Fred Ladd.

Ladd was an independent television producer who specialized in taking documentaries about wildlife filmed in Europe and editing them for broadcast on American TV. Frequently, the documentaries spanned between 30 and 50 minutes, meaning they could not fit into the 30- and 60-minute time slots networks demanded for their shows. Ladd reedited the European documentaries into lengths that could be shown on American TV. He also had the narrations dubbed into English.

Ladd also had some experience in animation. He helped produce English-language versions of several European cartoons, including the movie-length Belgian animation *Pinocchio in Outer Space*, which he recut and dubbed into English for American audiences.

Ladd was approached by NBC to look over some episodes of *Tetsuwan Atom* to see whether it could be packaged for audiences in the United States. Ladd immediately recognized the show's potential. He edited one of the episodes into a pilot, which is a trial version of a show that is tested in front of an audience. He said,

> *Sometime in 1963, NBC's representative in Tokyo saw a very, very limited action, adventure show on television about a little boy called* Tetsuwan Atom ... *NBC Enterprises, a division of the broadcast network, picked it up very cheap, not even knowing what they were buying. No one spoke Japanese. No one really understood it.*
>
> *They then tracked me down, knowing I had done a lot of cartoon dubbing as well as* Pinocchio in Outer Space, *and showed me a couple of episodes and asked me what I thought. As a result, I made a pilot, NBC saw it and said, "All right, do another one. We can sell this." I did and it became* Astro Boy.[9]

A Change in Style

NBC could not keep the translated name *Mighty Atom*—there was already a comic book hero in the United States by that name. Ladd changed his name to *Astro Boy*. This was the era in which the first American astronauts were being launched into space, and Ladd knew that a lot of public interest was already being shown in anything that sounded as though it involved adventures in space.

Instead of airing the show on NBC, network executives elected instead to syndicate the program, meaning they sold it station by station to their affiliates as well as to independent TV stations. Still, *Astro Boy* was aired in most major TV markets in the United States, and it proved to be popular among its young viewers. American producers soon imported more Mushi shows, including *Kimba the White Lion*, which featured the adventures of a young lion in Africa who protected the animals of his homeland; *Gigantor*, a story about a young boy's friendship with a giant crime-fighting robot; *Speed Racer*, which featured the adventures of a race car driver who frequently found himself caught up in intrigue involving spies, evil scientists, and assorted thugs; and *8 Man*, a series about a murdered detective given new life as a robot.

Despite the appeal of the early shows, anime did not take over American TV. For starters, the style of animation of the Japanese shows compared to the American-made animated shows such as *The Flintstones*, as well as the films produced by Disney, was not what American audiences were used to. Starting with *Kimba*, which was paid for in part by NBC, the Japanese shows were animated in color but obviously still produced on tight budgets. To save money, artists used fewer animation cels. As such, anime looked different when compared to American animation. In some scenes, it seemed as though the only parts of the character that were truly animated were the eyes and the mouth—the rest of the body stood rock-still against an indistinct background. Disney and other Western studios had more money available, so they used a more expensive technique called "full animation," which allowed images to have as many as 24 changes in one frame of film. Each frame of film lasts about one second, so when it was all viewed at high speed, the movements seemed very lifelike. In contrast, Japanese animators typically used the cheaper "shot on threes" technique, where one image would take up three frames. This made Japanese-animated characters appear to be moving more jerkily by comparison.

Also, the Japanese programs were heavily edited. In addition to the English dubbing, the editors Americanized the characters' names

Kimba the White Lion was the first anime to be produced in color.

and chopped out most references to Japanese culture—such as when characters ate with chopsticks, drank the Japanese rice wine known as sake, or bowed to one another in greeting. In addition, American animators had fallen under strict guidelines when it came to portraying violence in children's programming. There were no such rules in Japan, and as a result, anime often featured extremely violent acts. Those scenes were cut out of the American versions, which satisfied network censors but generally affected the story lines and made the plots choppy or hard to follow. Finally, in Japan, the stories were typically told as serials—each show was based on events and plot twists told in the previous week's show. In America, the shows were edited so the story could be related in a single episode. It is important to note that these standards of censorship continue today when it comes to anime broadcast on television for children. It is much easier for Westerners to find uncut anime through online streaming services.

The Lion King "Borrows" from Anime

Soon after Disney released *The Lion King* in 1994, anime fans discovered many similarities between the Disney animated film and an old Japanese TV series, *Kimba the White Lion*. For starters, the names of the two main characters were quite similar. In the TV series, Kimba was the main character; in the Disney film, the young lion cub destined to be king is named Simba. However, Kimba got his name after the show came to the United States. In the original version, his name was Leo, but there was already a famous cartoon lion with that name. Since *simba* is Swahili for "lion," translators planned to use that name for Kimba, but there were copyright conflicts there as well, so they changed it slightly.

The plots were also similar. Kimba and Simba were both robbed of their title by an evil lion. In the TV series, Kimba was helped by a wise old baboon and a talking bird; similar characters befriended Simba. Fred Ladd, the American producer who edited *Kimba* for American audiences, said, "There are inescapable comparisons."[1]

Executives from the Disney studio denied that they had borrowed liberally from the old *Kimba* show—a situation that could expose the studio to expensive lawsuits. *Kimba*'s originator, Osamu Tezuka, died before *The Lion King* was released, but American anime authority Frederik L. Schodt believed Tezuka would not be offended if he had known Disney borrowed elements from his story. "He would be chuckling," Schodt said. "He might find it flattering."[2]

1. Quoted in Ann Oldenburg, "The Lion King Shares a Jungle Crown," *USA Today*, July 14, 1994, p. D-1.
2. Quoted in Oldenburg, "The Lion King Shares a Jungle Crown."

An Important Series

While anime settled into a niche in American entertainment reserved for children, back in Japan, the animation industry had exploded. Unlike America, where animated shows had always been regarded as programming intended strictly for young children, Japanese teenagers and adults were also avid fans. Tezuka's Mushi Productions developed shows for older viewers, often adapting classical stories to anime. For example, Mushi produced anime versions of the Arabian series of folktales, *A Thousand and One Nights*, as well as *Cleopatra*, a story about the doomed Egyptian queen. Also, Mushi and its many competitors—since the early 1960s, dozens of new animation studios had opened in Japan—were now producing sophisticated science fiction and adventure dramas. In 1974, Japanese audiences had their first look at a TV series titled *Space Battleship Yamato*, in which an old World War II battleship, the *Yamato*, is converted into a spaceship that travels the galaxy searching for an anti-radiation device that will save Earth.

Space Battleship Yamato featured sophisticated scripts that were several steps beyond the simple stories of good versus evil that children could see on *Astro Boy* or *Speed Racer*. For example, the show resurrected the Japanese people's uncomfortable memories of World War II, suggesting that a weapon from the old Japanese Imperial Navy, the *Yamato*, could now be used to save Earth. In addition to the thought-provoking scripts, *Space Battleship Yamato* featured strong character development and a high quality of animation. American anime authorities Jonathan Clements and Helen McCarthy said,

> *Space Battleship Yamato [SBY] is one of the watersheds in anime history … [the show] contained a supremely strong story line. SBY changed the way TV programmers thought about science fiction; previously, it had been supposed that only very young audiences watched TV anime, and so there was no point in screening anything but giant-robot and [superhero] shows. The influence of the original series on a whole generation of Japanese animators is incredible.*[10]

Soon, other animated space dramas went into production. Among the shows that debuted on Japanese TV during this era were *Mazinger Z*, a series about the adventures of a flying mechanical warrior; *Captain Harlock*, which told of a pirate who did his buccaneering in a spaceship; and *Queen Millennia*, which related the story of an extraterrestrial queen who protected Earth from evil forces on her home planet.

The Rise of Anime in the West

At first, *Space Battleship Yamato* as well as the other animated science fiction shows were not broadcast on American TV. In fact, American audiences had no idea that anime had progressed beyond *Kimba the White Lion*, which, during the 1970s, was still being broadcast on American TV. However, things started changing in the late 1970s, thanks mostly to the development of the videocassette player.

Tapes of original Japanese anime started making their way into American markets. Some of the tapes were brought home by tourists, but other tapes were being stocked on "anime shelves" in videotape rental stores or were bought and sold at science fiction conventions. Even though the dialogue was in Japanese, many dedicated anime fans were able to follow the stories despite the language barrier. Some fans who were skilled in Japanese would translate the dialogue on their own and edit

The invention of the videocassette, which let people watch movies at home, was an important development in the spread of anime from the East to the West.

the tapes to have English subtitles on them so others could follow along better. These "fansubbed" movies were more widely available than movies that were subtitled by production companies. The absence of U.S.-based representation for many anime production companies meant there was very little authorized distribution; American companies often did not wish to license shows not marketable to children, so fans had to take matters into their own hands.

What is more, American fans discovered that anime was not just for kids. In a culture that was suddenly in love with science fiction—the first Star Wars film had premiered in 1977, ushering in a new era in science fiction entertainment—American fans discovered that anime was dominated by space adventures, many told on a teenage or adult level featuring romance, violence, and plots in which the lines between good and evil were often blurred.

Of course, American TV producers soon heard about the popularity of Japanese animation and started obtaining new anime for broadcast in the American market. Among the first of the new breed of anime shows to be featured on American TV was *Battle of the Planets*. The show, which debuted in 1978, told the story of five young heroes and their giant, birdlike spaceship that protected Earth from an evil alien named Gallacter. A year later, *Space Battleship Yamato* was imported for broadcast in the United States, although American producers changed the name to *Star Blazers*.

As in the *Astro Boy* era, the new shows underwent a considerable amount of editing. They were dubbed into English, and to satisfy the network censors, the violence was still being chopped out. Patten said,

> *Early anime fandom had a strongly evangelical fervor. Many fans did not mind watching untranslated anime videos for the visual drama alone. When* Battle of the Planets *and* Star Blazers *spread through syndication around America, there was the thrill of being "in the know" about what the original anime was like. Anime fans would show videos of the unedited Japanese episodes and point out all the scenes of violence that had been censored.*[11]

Indeed, American anime fans knew the best parts of the Japanese shows were being cut out of the versions they were seeing on their TV sets in the United States. They also knew that the shows that were being produced in Japan often ventured into topics that were far more thought-provoking than what the American producers had chosen to import. For example, a show that hit Japanese airwaves in 1982 was titled *Xabungle*, which was something of a space comedy. In the series, the main character Xabungle (the name is taken from the Japanese word for "bungler") is an inept robot on a quest to find the truth about the death of his father. He engages in many humorous battles, often set against a background that resembled the American Wild West. While audiences laughed, they also had to ponder some significant themes. In Xabungle's world, a class struggle existed between the

Subbed or Dubbed?

A long-running argument among anime fans is about which is better: a subtitled movie, where the dialogue is spoken in Japanese by the original voice actors and the English translation can be read at the bottom of the screen, or a dubbed one, where American actors re-record the dialogue in English. The website TV Tropes summed up just a few of the arguments for and against each of these practices:

> *Subtitling has many advantages: It allows for an extremely accurate translation, including quirks of the original language that play a role in the plot, while allowing you to hear the original actors' performances. It renders the show accessible to the deaf or hard of hearing ... Some fansubbers even include notes in the subtitles that help explain certain cultural references or jokes that might not otherwise be properly understood by a non-native audience ...*
>
> *On the other hand ... subtitlers will often trim dialogue due to subtitle line-length restrictions ... Additionally, bored fansubbers will occasionally decide to alter the script to make it more "adult" ... Hearing actors speaking one's native language also allows the audience to catch subtle non-verbal parts of a performance, which many times is part of the "authentic" viewing experience the original was shooting for. Subtitles can cover up important parts of the image or switch too quickly to be read by everyone ... In addition, subtitles—particularly for unofficial fansubs—are sometimes criticized for being too literal; a well-made dub can preserve the spirit of a joke or reference, even while replacing the actual line.*[1]

In the end, it comes down to a fan's personal preference. Some people prefer subbed anime, others prefer dubbed, and some prefer to choose based on how well the subtitling or dubbing was done.

1. "Subbing vs. Dubbing," TV Tropes. tvtropes.org/pmwiki/pmwiki.php/Main/SubbingVersusDubbing.

privileged Innocents, who lived in luxury inside a glass dome, and the lowly Civilians, who had to perform manual labor outside the dome in the hostile environment of the planet Zola.

Another show that debuted on Japanese TV in 1982 was *Macross*, which told the story of a team of young heroes who repair and pilot a giant starship that had crashed into Earth. The show was based on the premise that the aliens who constructed the starship, the Zentraedi, were a warlike people descended from the same ancestors as humans. While audiences pondered the question of whether humans were headed down the same path as the Zentraedi, there was a lot more in *Macross* to keep viewers occupied. The show featured a heavy dose of romance among its characters. It was also a musical. Each week, one of the characters performed a song; later, albums of *Macross* hits were sold to the show's fans.

In 1985, American TV producer Carl Macek imported *Macross* for American viewers. In the United States, the show was aired under the title *Robotech*. Macek actually combined *Macross* with two other anime shows and had the final version dubbed into English. Nevertheless, he left in the romance, the thought-provoking themes, and the violence—by then, network TV censors were not quite as strict as they had been in the 1960s and 1970s. Macek said,

> Macross *has elements that are completely unknown to American TV cartoons, but are common to comic-book readers and moviegoers. It has a realistic war story in which some of the major good guys get killed. There are robots and space battles, but the plot is really a soap opera that emphasizes the continuing relationships between people. Earth's civilization gets wiped out about three-quarters through the series, not just to show off spectacular violence but as an important, serious plot development ...* Macross *is an animated cartoon that fans who think they've outgrown TV cartoons have been waiting for without knowing it.*[12]

Akira

Robotech was followed by other imported shows that greatly expanded the anime available to American audiences. Throughout the 1980s, anime developed a cult-like following. Entrepreneurs established magazines to keep fans updated on the adventures of top anime characters as well as news about the shows and studios. Bookstores stocked manga titles. Organizations of fans started forming, particularly on college campuses. The biggest group organized during the 1980s was the Earth Defense Command Animation Society, which held the first national anime convention in Dallas, Texas, in 1990. An even bigger convention, Anime Expo—known among fans as the "AX"—is held annually in Los Angeles, California. Attendance at this event has increased dramatically over the years. In 2006, around 41,000 anime fans attended the four-day event; in 2016, the convention celebrated its 25th anniversary and was attended by a record-breaking 100,000 people.

With an established audience in America for anime, the movie industry found room for Japanese animation in American theaters. A major anime film featured in American movie theaters was the futuristic supernatural thriller *Akira*, which was released in 1988 and was based on a 1982 manga. The film told of a postapocalyptic world that is starting to rebuild itself when an old nemesis returns—a biological weapon named Akira. The film is set in 2019, a time when biker gangs rule the city streets and the government is manipulated by evil corporate interests—themes well beyond the simple stories found in *Astro Boy* and *Kimba* or even the save-the-planet plots of *Space Battleship Yamato*.

Akira was also a technological achievement. The filmmakers were among the first anime producers to use computers to create some of the animation in the film, a process that had been used around the same time in the United States by Disney, which had used computers in the production of *The Little Mermaid*. "*Akira* is almost single-handedly responsible for the early 1990s boom in anime in the English language," said Clements and McCarthy. "*Akira* was a visual tour-de-force, including experiments in digital … animation that were to stun audiences worldwide, enjoying greater success abroad than in its country of origin."[13]

American film critic Janet Maslin praised the film's director, Katsuhiro Otomo, for the quality of the animation. She wrote,

> *Mr. Otomo and his army of highly skilled animators are at their best for conjuring up wildly turbulent special effects, which are rendered with great energy and ingenuity. Akira presents dozens of variations on the image of billowing smoke, in every imaginable range of colors. And when its characters hurtle through space, they do it with breathtaking energy. Among the film's typically strange and arresting sequences are one that shows tiny nursery toys transformed into huge, terrifying monsters, and another in which huge, frightening gobs of protoplasm spring out of the body of a frightened victim.*[14]

Akira *changed the way anime was produced.*

Anime Wins an Oscar

There was no question that anime had grown into a commercially successful venture in the United States and that films such as *Akira* proved that anime could also compete on an artistic level against American-produced animation. At the 2003 Academy Awards, the film *Spirited Away* was awarded the Oscar for best animated feature, beating out such popular films as *Lilo & Stitch* and *Ice Age*. Directed by Hayao Miyazaki, one of Japan's most influential anime filmmakers, *Spirited Away* was the first anime film to win Hollywood's most prestigious award. The film tells the story of a young girl named Chihiro who enters a world of

Spirited Away was the first anime film to win an Academy Award. It was directed by Hayao Miyazaki (shown on the next page), one of Japan's most famous and influential filmmakers.

spirits where she must save her family with the help of a young boy who can turn into a dragon.

American film critic Roger Ebert called the movie "the best animated film of recent years."[15] He praised the production values of *Spirited Away* and the filmmakers for maintaining an atmosphere of Japanese culture in the film—largely missing since the *Astro Boy* days. Most of the film's action takes place in a Japanese bathhouse, an institution for bathing and relaxation that is common in Japan but unknown in America. Also, the filmmakers drop in many other references to Japanese culture. For example, Chihiro's parents turn into pigs while eating large amounts of food they find at a traditional open-air restaurant.

There is no question that anime has become part of the entertainment culture in America over the past several decades. In many of the years since *Spirited Away* won an Academy Award, other anime films have received nominations as well. This list includes *Howl's Moving Castle* in 2005, a story of a young hatter named Sophie who is turned into an old woman by a witch's curse, and *The Tale of Princess Kaguya* in 2014, a film based on the folktale *The Tale of the Bamboo Cutter*. In both cases, the films were recognized both for their storytelling and their artwork.

Although neither of these films took home the Oscar, they were critically acclaimed. For example, Nicholas Rapold of the *New York Times* praised

The Tale of Princess Kaguya, calling it "[e]xquisitely drawn with both watercolor delicacy and a brisk sense of line."[16]

There is no question that anime will continue to be a part of the entertainment culture in America for years to come. Many anime and manga have been adapted into live-action movies, including *Death Note* in 2006, *Speed Racer* in 2008, and the anime-inspired *The Last Airbender* in 2010.

Ghost in the Shell was adapted from a 1995 anime about a cyborg policewoman and her partner. The 2017 live-action version, which stars Scarlett Johansson, received mixed reactions from fans. Some were excited to see a live-action version of an anime they enjoyed, but others were concerned that the remake would not do the original justice. The movie particularly came under fire for casting Johansson as the main character, since she is white and her character in the original is Japanese. Director Rupert Sanders defended his casting decision, stating that Johansson was the best actress for the role, but the debate among fans continues.

CHAPTER THREE

Why Anime Stands Out

Even a casual viewer can immediately see stylistic differences between anime and the style of animation found in the United States. These style differences are what make anime so unique.

One of the most iconic features of anime for Western viewers is the design of the eyes. This style uses large, round eyes that can be either simply or intricately drawn. This characteristic was the invention of Tezuka, who fell upon the technique partially because of money constraints. Tight budgets required artists to tell their stories in as few animation cels as possible. Instead of words to convey characters' feelings, Tezuka used their facial expressions. Most notably, large eyes could show a wide range of emotions, such as fear, joy, and rage.

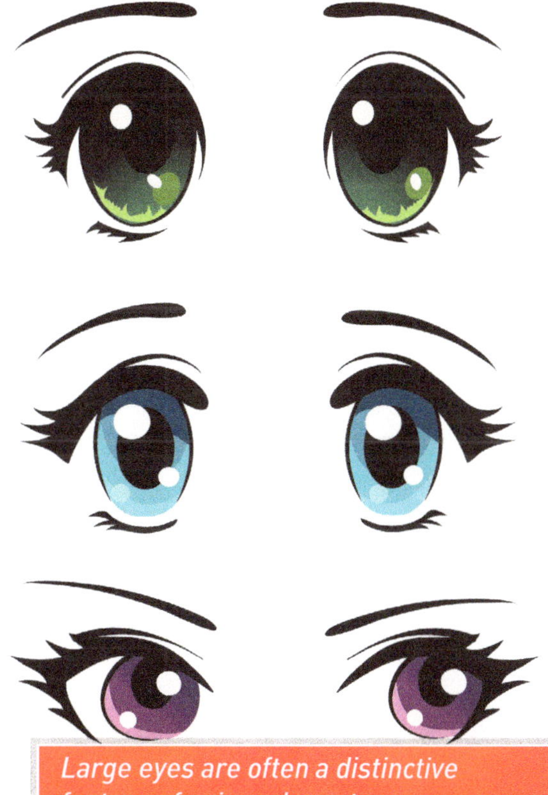

Large eyes are often a distinctive feature of anime characters.

Tezuka drew inspiration from Disney movies, which often show animated characters with unnaturally large eyes to make them seem more innocent and lovable. Additionally, recent studies have found that Japanese people tend to look at people's eyes for clues about how they are feeling, while Americans look at people's mouths. All of these factors may explain why the eyes of anime characters have historically been drawn so large.

Other unique details can be found in anime and manga. It is these details that set anime apart from forms of commercial art in other countries. Creators of anime have worked diligently over the years to craft a vibrant and energetic style that is specific to Japanese culture and its sensibilities.

Characters from the long-running manga and anime series Dragon Ball Z, *shown here, still maintain the iconic character designs of series creator Akira Toriyama.*

Miyazaki's Story

The first anime director to win an Academy Award, Hayao Miyazaki, is one of Japan's most influential and successful filmmakers. Born in 1941, Miyazaki turned to art at an early age. His family owned a factory that manufactured parts for airplanes. As a child, he would accompany his father to the plant, where he enjoyed drawing the planes. His interest in art led to a career in anime.

After graduating from college in 1963, Miyazaki found a job in an animation studio. In 1985, he founded his own production company, Studio Ghibli, which has become one of Japan's most successful anime studios.

Many of Ghibli's films feature young girls as the central characters. Faced with overwhelming challenges as well as personal crises, Miyazaki's heroines always find a way to succeed. Before releasing *Spirited Away*, Miyazaki directed *Princess Mononoke*, a story set in medieval Japan in which guardian spirits must protect a forest from humans, as well as *Kiki's Delivery Service*, a story about a young witch in training who regains her magical powers when she becomes independent and self-reliant. Miyazaki's strong female characters were ahead of their time and eventually influenced Disney animators.

The Anime Spirit

One of the reasons anime and manga stand apart from movie and comic art produced in the United States is an attention to detail common in Japanese culture but often sacrificed in American animation. Christopher Hart, an American cartoonist and art teacher, said anime and manga artists often try to reproduce the tiniest elements in their characters or in the backgrounds of the scenes:

> *What makes anime such an instantly recognizable style? Certainly, the character design is unique, focusing on large eyes and subtle features. But beneath it all is a philosophy that captures the essence of the anime spirit.*
>
> *Western-style animation expresses itself primarily through movement. The more a character moves, the "better" the animation is thought to be. So, it's not surprising that animation producers in the West typically redesign comic book characters for television, simplifying them to allow for greater movement. Although anime characters are*

also licensed from comic books, emphasis is placed on retaining the integrity of the original comic. The detail and subtlety in the drawings are not sacrificed to allow for greater movement. As a result, anime has the appearance of a real comic book come to life![17]

One of the reasons that Japanese anime artists have decided to retain

In Japan, foods, objects, and animals are frequently drawn with eyes, mouths, and blushing cheeks to make them cute, or kawaii.

Tezuka's style for drawing eyes is that it makes the characters look cute. Japanese culture places even more emphasis on cuteness than Western culture does. This is called *kawaii*, a word that means "cute" or "lovable." Both men and women participate in *kawaii* culture in Japan, so it is not uncommon to see men with stuffed animals or backpacks with cartoons on them. The widespread popularity of characters such as Hello Kitty illustrates how much influence *kawaii* culture has. So, in a culture that values cuteness, it should come as no surprise that in anime and manga, artists take steps to make sure their characters retain an element of cuteness—even in stories that are otherwise punctuated by violence and end-of-the-world themes.

Apart from the eyes, the other most obvious feature found in the faces of Japanese anime characters is that to Americans, they rarely appear to be Japanese. Most characters found in anime or manga appear to be of Western ethnicity. This style dates back to the earliest years of anime in the 1950s. At the time, anime was in competition with live-action films for ticket sales among Japanese audiences. Because the Japanese live-action movie companies operated under extremely tight budgets, the films had to be produced in Japan using Japanese actors. As such, the plots were limited to stories about domestic life in Japan. Anime artists found that by using an art technique they called *mukokuseki*, meaning "without nationality," they could give them an international flavor and center the stories in any country they desired. *Mukokuseki* combines traits of many different ethnic groups so the characters do not appear to belong to any particular time or place. This helped the anime producers lure Japanese audiences, who were eager to see movies about other places. It became an important part of the anime style of art. Writer Latonya Pennington explained,

> *This technique is used by creators to make bold anime that isn't associated with the uniform culture of Japan.*
>
> *"In Japan, white is not the default," writer Brian Ashcraft explains … "Japanese is. Thus, there is no need for them to 'look Asian,' because no matter how ridiculous the characters look, everyone will assume they are Japanese."*
>
> *In other words, Japanese anime attempts to stand out in a monolithic culture where everyone is expected to be the same. Anime is the spot of color you'd notice in a sea of grey.*[18]

Anime's Distinctive Style

The hair colors found on anime and manga characters are another example of *mukokuseki*. Most Japanese people have black hair or very dark brown hair. In anime, hair colors vary widely—from dark tones to blond to red, green, and purple.

Outside Japan, comic artists frequently use hair color to identify characters so that a reader can easily recognize a character in the scene. Since manga artists were originally restricted to working in black and white, they compensated by drawing distinct hairstyles. Today, some manga is published in color, but even in color manga, characters are drawn with outlandish hairstyles—it is simply a holdover from the days when the manga artists were forced to work strictly in black and white.

To an anime artist, hair can be used for purposes other than to identify a character or to help illustrate the character's personality. Anime artists have found they can use hair to convey emotions, action, and drama. Poitras said,

> *The movement of a character's hair is quite noticeable in anime. Hair flows in the breeze, moves when the character shifts*

Pokémon's Revival

Millions of young American children have been caught up in the Pokémon craze that landed in the United States in 1998. Conceived first as a video game—players caught a series of characters known as "pocket monsters"—the characters eventually evolved into comic books as well as a feature film and a series broadcast on American TV. In 1999, the first Pokémon comic book published in the United States sold more than a million copies. The exact reason for its huge popularity is unknown, but according to tech website VentureBeat, it may be due to "its multimedia content strategy, its strong focus on collection, and its paper-rock-scissors battle mechanics,"[1] as well as the fact that kids felt like they were part of something their parents did not understand.

In July 2016, *Pokémon Go* came out and started another immediate craze. The game was popular with older people who had grown up with Pokémon in the late 1990s as well as younger fans. This interactive game involved catching virtual Pokémon in real places using smartphones and other devices. The fact that it combined Pokémon with the outdoors made it intensely appealing to people of all ages.

1. Jeff Grubb, "Why Pokémon Still Matters 20 Years Later," VentureBeat, August 9, 2016. venturebeat.com/2016/08/09/why-pokemon-still-matters-20-years-later/.

Pokémon Go *restarted the Pokémon craze in the United States.*

suddenly, or comes to a halt. It gets wild during battle, and settles during a moment of stillness. A character may be pensive, with eyes cast downward, and a small lock of hair will come loose from behind an ear at a visually interesting moment. "Hair action" thus adds to the atmosphere of scenes and enhances the behaviors and feelings of the characters. It requires more complex cels and makes the anime more expensive, but the effect is a powerful one and adds much to one's viewing pleasure.[19]

In anime, movement also affects how the characters are portrayed as they walk, run, and make other motions. For example, anime characters bend low when they run, which helps create the illusion of speed. However, when they walk, many anime characters walk tall and with authority. Anime artists often find that they can best animate conversations if their characters are walking while they are talking. Hart said, "Whereas the typical anime run is portrayed as an all-out panic, the anime walk is restrained. The body is upright and stiff."[20]

Often in anime, a character's distinct look or style is used for emotional purposes. For example, a character may increase in size in order to show anger. Another example of this technique is a character suddenly losing the detail in their face, the effect being that vagueness conveys fear, shame, or sadness.

Backgrounds of anime scenes have also become much more sophisticated in recent years. In the *Astro Boy* days, a background was essentially a painted picture—the scene never changed, although the characters moved their feet. As their budgets grew, Japanese animators improved the backgrounds

Anime characters have a wide variety of hairstyles. These are used to identify the characters and show their personality.

in the scenes. Anime artists have found they can give the stories more depth if they provide a sense of movement in the backgrounds. Poitras said,

> *Overall, Japanese backgrounds are more likely to be in motion and to change and turn. Obviously, this costs more money, which is why a lot of American studios avoid the effect. Not all anime uses a dynamic background, but much of it does, along with other cinematic effects like pan shots, angles, distance shots, scenes where the focus between the foreground and background changes, and so on.*[21]

Manga's Vast Reach

In Japan, comic art is not only drawn differently than in America, it is also read differently. Japanese manga is read by fans who range from young children to adults; as such, it is written and drawn on different levels. Each genre has its own category. For example, boys between the ages of 6 and 18 are likely to read titles known as *shonen*, which is the Japanese word for "boy." *Shonen* titles predominantly feature action and adventure stories. *Shonen* is by far the most popular manga in Japan, with several magazines devoted to the genre. The largest is *Weekly Shonen Jump*, a weekly with a circulation of around 2 million readers. In comparison, America's largest magazine, *TIME*, which features news and commentary on current events, has a circulation of about 3 million readers a week.

Young girls tend to read *shojo*, which is the Japanese word for "girl." Readers of *shojo* are generally under 12. *Shojo* stories focus on strong relationships among the female protagonists. One of the most popular *shojo* series is *Peach Girl*, which has been adapted into an anime series and even a live-action stage play. *Peach Girl* tells the story of Momo, a blond-haired teenage girl who must endure the taunts, rumor-passing, and backstabbing of the other girls in her high school.

Girls over 12 often read *shonen ai*,which means "boy love" stories. These stories focus on romantic relationships among the male protagonists. One of the most popular *shonen ai* series is *Gravitation*, which has also been adapted into an anime series. *Gravitation* tells the story of the young musicians of a struggling rock band.

Men over the age of 18 often read *seinen*, or "adult," manga. In *seinen* manga, the violence is quite graphic and the skirts worn by the female characters tend to be quite short. There are dozens of successful *seinen* titles and several publications with large circulations that specialize in *seinen* manga. One of the most popular *seinen* series in Japan and the United States is *One Punch Man*, a chronicle of a superhero who is so strong that he can defeat an enemy with just one punch.

Women over the age of 18 tend to read *josei*, which is a Japanese word for "adult women." *Josei* manga generally centers on contemporary stories of women dealing with crises in their relationships and professional lives. One of the most successful *josei* series in Japan is *Paradise Kiss*, which tells the story of a young model named Yukari who must deal with the cutthroat world of high fashion. *Paradise Kiss* is also a popular anime series on Japanese TV.

Some manga is available in electronic form for e-readers.

Different than American Comics

Josei, *seinen*, and the other categories of manga are available on the shelves of bookstores in America. American readers will find them much fatter than typical comic books and even heftier than English-language graphic novels. Manga titles sometimes span several hundred pages.

Comic book readers may be used to square or rectangular frames that follow a standard format. In contrast, manga panels "are often set up like frames of a film, showing the progression of movements to give the reader a sense of time and action, and at times, the panels run together or are not used at all."[22]

In addition to panels of a different size and shape, new fans of manga should be aware that when they first pick a manga title off the shelf, they may be in for something of a surprise: The book is likely to open from the "wrong" side.

That is because the Japanese read from right to left. Although the books are translated into English, most publishers will keep the right-to-left orientation with a friendly note on the last page of the volume showing readers the correct way to read it. At first, American readers may find it difficult to follow the stories, but most manga fans quickly train their eyes to follow the action.

Some manga titles are published in a left-to-right format. This involves the practice known as "flipping," in which the images are printed backward from the original. Most of the time, the transition will be seamless, but occasionally, humorous little details emerge. For example, a reader may notice a car's steering wheel on the wrong side of the vehicle. A thug whom the artist has named "Lefty" may seem to always use his right hand.

However, manga that is published in the United States is generally not flipped; it is meant to be read the way other Western books are. Starting in 2007, HarperCollins, one of America's largest book publishers, collaborated with a Japanese manga publisher, Tokyopop, to produce a new series of titles featuring the work of American authors. The first author whose work was adapted into a manga format was Meg Cabot, the author of the Princess Diaries and Avalon High series of books for young readers. Other American publishers, including Random House and Simon & Schuster, have also established their own manga divisions or struck deals with Japanese publishers to distribute manga in America.

Jane Friedman, the former chief executive officer of HarperCollins, said she has long wanted to start a manga division at the New York–based publisher but realized that her company lacked the experience to produce its own manga titles.

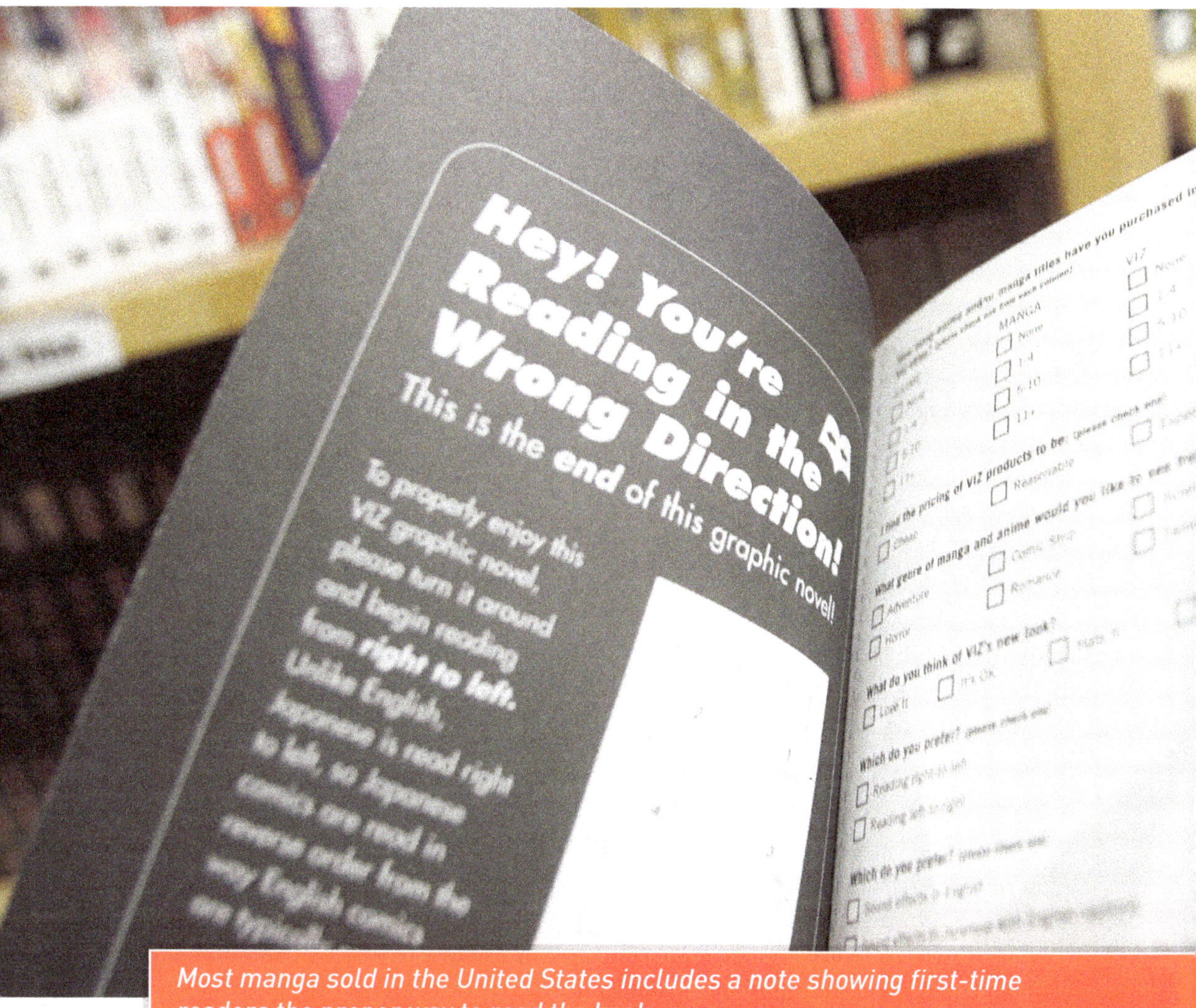

Most manga sold in the United States includes a note showing first-time readers the proper way to read the book.

She pointed out that there are few manga artists working in the United States today, and that is why the participation of a Tokyo-based publisher was necessary to adapt U.S. titles into the format. Meanwhile, she said, HarperCollins owns the rights to a wealth of literature for young readers that have until now been unavailable to the Japanese manga publishers.

The collaboration between the two publishing companies lasted until 2011, when Tokyopop signed a new deal with Diamond Comics Distributors. However, manga versions of some novels can still be found in bookstores and libraries across the country.

Cosplay Etiquette

Anime fans sometimes enjoy dressing up as their favorite characters when they go to conventions, or cons. This is known as cosplay, short for "costume play." Outfits can be relatively simple or extremely elaborate. Many people put a lot of time, effort, and money into their costumes. People who go to a con should remember to be respectful of cosplayers and ask permission before they touch parts of the costume or take pictures of the cosplayer.

People who are thinking about cosplay have many options to choose from. There are thousands of characters from anime, manga, and live-action movies. Gender is generally not a barrier to cosplay; many women dress up as their favorite male characters, and some men dress as their favorite female characters. However, cosplayers do need to be aware of the issue of race. Although anime characters are understood to be Japanese, they are typically drawn without racially distinguishing features, leaving it generally accepted that a white person may cosplay as an anime character. In contrast, it is never acceptable in any facet of society for a white person to present themselves as a person of color by painting their skin or altering facial features to resemble another race.

Many cosplayers put a lot of time and effort into their costumes to make them look as authentic as possible.

CHAPTER FOUR

Anime's Strong Female Roles

In the early 1990s, the Japanese show *Sailor Moon* made its debut for American audiences and quickly became a success. Starting out as a manga series in Japan, the show quickly transitioned to television as an animated series. *Sailor Moon* features more than 200 episodes, three feature films, live action interpretations, and even a Broadway-style musical.

Sailor Moon centers around a teenage girl named Serena and her extraordinary power to transform into the heroine Sailor Moon in order to fight the forces of evil. Assisting Serena in these battles are her fellow Sailor Scouts, all of whom are named after planets. The characters are all strong females, so not only can girls relate to the show's characters, they can also view Sailor Moon and her fellow warriors as role models. The girls of *Sailor Moon* are strong, intelligent and brave. They accomplish heroic deeds without the help of their boyfriends, fathers, or any other males and do not need to be rescued by anyone. In addition, the show goes beyond the surface to portray the Sailor Scouts as real people, with real problems and emotions. In the series, as the stories unfold, Serena and her friends grow and mature.

The characters of *Sailor Moon*, as well the characters of many other anime films and TV shows, differ greatly from the female characters in some Western animation. In anime, women are often equal to men,

Sailor Moon *features strong, independent female characters.*

while in many Western animated TV shows and movies, women have needed men to save them. There are many examples of this difference. For instance, in *Snow White and the Seven Dwarfs*, the title character needs a man to save her from a witch's curse.

In anime, female characters often save themselves. In *Sailor Moon*, the title character and her all-girl team defend the Earth against numerous enemies, even when outnumbered and overpowered, by relying on their strength, love, and friendship. In the 1997 film *Princess Mononoke*, a teenage girl raised by wolves fights to protect the wildlife of her forest. The protagonist is both a leader and a brave warrior. For years, *Princess Mononoke* was the highest grossing film in Japan. Male and female audiences of all ages were drawn to the wolf princess, regardless of the fact that this character was only secondary to the plot. However, in the early days of anime's jump to the West, producers tended to export shows targeted at boys, such as *Speed Racer*, since they were seen as more universal. This attitude persists today; TV and movie producers often justify the underrepresentation of women in the media by saying that boys do not want to watch things that star strong female characters, but *Princess Mononoke* and countless other works prove this statement false.

Women's Growing Role

Some Westerners believe the Japanese think women should be quiet and submissive, so they are surprised to see Japanese media that features strong female characters. However, this view of Japanese women is a myth, according to Price. She said the Japanese Shinto religion respects women and reserves an important place for them in society. There is no question that Japanese animators bring their beliefs to the drawing table. Price said,

> *Unlike much of Western folklore and heroics, many of the ancient Japanese tales of gods and demons are composed of female deities and spirits. Japanese history is also dominated by powerful empresses, priestesses, writers and artisans. As a result, anime is chock full of female protagonists and villains. Contrary to the subservient geisha stereotype of Japanese women, Japanese society is quite tolerant of strong women in the family and the workplace, quite possibly because ancient history and Shinto belief are filled with powerful heroines that played prominent roles in the shaping of Japan.*[23]

It is not surprising that *Sailor Moon* and similar shows were a hit in Japan before they arrived in America.

Unlike most Western religions, Japanese belief systems such as Tao and Shinto feature powerful goddesses. This may help explain why anime includes more strong female characters than Western animation.

Girls and women are dedicated readers of manga in Japan—and not just the *shojo*, *shonen ai*, and *josei* categories written specifically for female readers. Girls and women also read a lot of manga written for both sexes or written specifically for boys and men. With so many dedicated female readers, it is obvious that the manga publishers would risk losing fans if female characters were portrayed only as helpless victims who need strong male heroes to rescue them.

Gender Issues in Anime

Although many anime and manga feature strong female characters, problems still exist in some series. As in Western comics, the hypersexualization of girls and women is a problem. Johanna Draper Carlson, the editor of the review website Comics Worth Reading, said, "When you had mostly boys and men making comics, you had comics made mainly for boys and men. Then you end up with teen-girl superheroes who are drawn like Victoria's Secret models."[24]

Naoko Takeuchi

The creator of *Sailor Moon* never intended to be an artist. Born in 1967, Naoko Takeuchi majored in chemistry in college. After receiving her degree from Kyoritsu Yakka University in Tokyo, Takeuchi found a job as a pharmacist at Keio Hospital in the Japanese city of Ise. She was always interested in art, though, and started drawing as a young girl.

As a college student, she produced her first professional manga title, *Love Call*, which was published in a major manga magazine in Japan. She also developed a manga series, *Cherry Project*, which told the story of young figure skaters.

While working at the hospital pharmacy, the editor of a manga magazine suggested she develop a series about teenage girls who wear sailor uniforms, which is a standard dress code for junior high and high school girls in Japan. The series Takeuchi created—a story about a girl with magical powers—was originally titled *Codename Sailor V* and made its debut in 1991. After refining the concept, Takeuchi developed the series *Sailor Moon*, which debuted a year later in manga and anime. Takeuchi later said that she accepted the suggestion of the characters wearing sailor uniforms because she knew junior high and high school can be difficult years for girls, and she felt they needed a hero who would represent them in manga and anime.

However, even female manga artists often draw their female characters with exaggerated figures, and they sometimes wear costumes that barely cover their bodies. Some anime objectifies these women; they do not have personalities, and they simply exist for the male characters and viewers to look at. According to writer Alexis Brazier, this "isolates many female viewers and distracts the audience from the show's desired narrative."[25] Additionally, sometimes the personalities of the women in anime are stereotyped for a male audience. Brazier explained,

> *Another frequent trope is for female characters to elicit 'moe'—that feeling of burning passion otakus [people who have an obsession with anime] are known to have for two dimensional characters. Usually this feeling is accomplished via cutesy mannerisms and exhibiting traditionally female stereotypes. Traditionally as in 'ideal woman in the 1940s,' as in 'someone who will love me immediately and unconditionally, do all the housework, make me sandwiches and have no real desires or goals that interfere with my own.' These characters are unrealistic, and frustrating to watch as a woman who knows these characters only exist to be [idealized].*[26]

Women and girls who see female characters constantly being portrayed as stupid or helpless, or as people whose only purpose is to be appealing to men, generally feel frustrated and upset because these characters often reflect the way society views real women. According to Anne Toole, the creator of the female-centered comic *Crystal Cadets*, "Sometimes it's as simple as seeing some commonality between yourself and what's on the page that can make you feel better about yourself. It's nice to be acknowledged and to be recognized that you exist in the world."[27]

This is also an issue for people of color; members of the lesbian, gay, bisexual, and transgender (LGBT+) community, as well as people with disabilities. Anime and manga tend to be more inclusive of these groups than Western animation, which may be one reason why they have become so popular in the West. For example, in addition to *shonen ai*, there is a category called *shojo ai*, which focuses on romantic relationships between women. These categories have been popular in Japan for years. However, there are still issues with the way some anime and manga portray these underrepresented groups.

Anime that shows same-sex couples has been popular in Japan for years. In contrast, very few Western animators include LGBT+ characters, even today.

Braver and More Aware

Sailor Moon and *Paradise Kiss* are both drawn by female manga artists. While American comic book publishers are just starting to recruit women writers and artists, Japanese manga and anime have long been written and drawn by women who are among the country's most successful artists. Poitras said, "Women play a major role in the industry as writers, artists, and animators—far beyond what is seen in other countries—and this shows in the kinds of programs being made."[28] *Paradise Kiss* is written and drawn by Ai Yazawa, who has produced more than a dozen successful manga series, all aimed at female audiences.

Among the most successful manga artists in Japan are four women who compose their manga under the name Clamp. Clamp started out as a circle of 11 art students who got together to compose *doujinshi*, which is amateur manga. Typically, *doujinshi* takes the adventures of popular manga characters beyond where their published stories leave off, similar to fan fiction.

Some *doujinshi* artists graduate into the professional ranks, and that is what happened to Clamp in 1989. After some initial successes in publishing professional manga, seven of the artists dropped out to forge their own careers. The four remaining Clamp members evolved into a very successful team; they were responsible for the production of more than 20 well-read manga series, many of which have been adapted into anime. Many of their anime titles have been dubbed into English and imported into the United States, where they are available in DVD format. "Clamp have been an integral part of the manga explosion that's occurred in the U.S. over the past several years," said Dallas Middaugh, former executive with the American publisher Random House. "Their fluid, dramatic artwork and storytelling struck a strong chord with male and female manga readers."[29]

One of Clamp's most popular series is *Tsubasa*, which has sold more than a million copies in the United States. The series has also been adapted into anime, which has been made available for sale in the United States on DVD. *Tsubasa* tells the story of four young adventurers who travel into other dimensions to retrieve the feathers from the wings of a princess spirit, who will die without them. Like Serena of *Sailor Moon*, the princess spirit of *Tsubasa*, a character named Sakura, is also presented as a very realistic girl who grows and matures as the series progresses. In fact, Clamp adapted Sakura into *Tsubasa* from one of its other anime and manga series, which was titled *Cardcaptor Sakura* and aimed at younger children. In *Cardcaptor Sakura*, 10-year-old Sakura discovers her powers when she accidentally releases evil spirits from a deck of cards. In the series, she is charged with the task of retrieving the spirits and returning them to the deck. Dr. Rachel Cantrell explained the appeal of this series:

> Cardcaptor Sakura *became a global hit essentially because it provided its female readers with a protagonist to whom they could relate intensely. Whether through her inner struggles with power and agency or through her*

emerging maturity in exploring love, Sakura becomes a character to whom readers could relate. The series' multicultural approach has made it appealing to preadolescent girls around the world. In addition, the series … models acceptance for same-sex relationships and provides a safe universe in which sexual identity can be explored.[30]

The strong, diverse characters in anime have inspired some Western animators. In *Avatar: The Last Airbender*, an anime-inspired TV series that aired from 2005 to 2008, the characters Katara and Toph Beifong are both powerful benders—people with a mastery of one of the four elements (earth, air, water, or fire). They work with the male characters but do not often need to be saved by them. They are both portrayed as women of color, and Toph is blind. Rather than keeping her from using her powers, her blindness makes her even better at earthbending.

Disabled Characters in Anime and Manga

In addition to its strong female role models, anime has a history of including disabled or ill characters who are still powerful and capable. Some examples include:

- Edward Elric, who has a mechanical arm and leg in *Fullmetal Alchemist*
- Ukitake, who has a serious lung condition in *Bleach*
- Ayase Sinomiya in *Guilty Crown,* who feels her wheelchair makes her unique
- Komugi, a talented young blind girl in *Hunter x Hunter*
- Nicolas Brown, a deaf man with extraordinary strength in *Gangsta*
- Kouyama Mitsuki, a 12-year-old girl who achieves her dream of becoming a pop star despite being diagnosed with throat cancer in *Full Moon o Sagashite*
- Rika Harada, a woman who runs her own design company despite being disabled in a car accident in *Honey & Clover*

Tracking Gender Inequality

The characters in manga frequently change in some way. Sometimes, the change is slow and takes place over the entire series, showing the characters growing and maturing in response to their experiences. Other times, the change is sudden and dramatic, often occurring through some kind of magic. One manga character who undergoes a dramatic transformation is Ranma Saotome, the featured character in the series *Ranma 1/2*. The series, which confronts women's issues head-on, was created by Rumiko Takahashi, one of the most successful manga artists in Japan. Fans of her work have bought more than 100 million copies of her manga titles, making her one of the wealthiest women in Japan. Many of Takahashi's titles have also been adapted into anime. Takahashi's titles have run the full spectrum of manga and anime genres: science fiction stories, martial arts dramas, mythological adventures, romantic tales, and coming-of-age stories.

One of Takahashi's best-known titles is *Inuyasha*, in which a teenage girl befriends a half-demon and travels back in time to help recover the pieces of a shattered jewel of power. However, *Ranma 1/2* is Takaski's older and more widely circulated series. In *Ranma 1/2*, which is a manga series, anime series, and feature film, the main character falls into a magical spring; when he emerges, Ranma finds that he changes into a girl whenever he is splashed with cold water. He changes back after he is splashed with hot water. As a girl, Ranma encounters discrimination, as well as unwanted sexual advances from teenage boys. However, when he fights as a girl, he employs techniques of cunning, intelligence, agility, and speed he does not think of using when he fights as a boy.

Fighting as a girl sometimes causes him trouble. When Ranma wins a martial arts competition as a girl, he faces bitterness from his male friends because they still do not believe his fighting ability measures up to what he could accomplish as a male fighter. Susan J. Napier said, "Although he wins in the end, his friends have little confidence in him because they are aware that even his martial arts expertise may not make up for his female limitations. Ranma's girlishness thus adds an extra tension to an already intense action sequence."[31]

Ranma 1/2 has never received broadcast or theatrical exposure in the United States, but episodes are available on video and DVD in America as well as other countries. *Ranma 1/2* is intended as a comedy, but there is no question that the issues confronted in the series are taken very seriously by contemporary girls and women.

Another female artist who tackles questions of gender inequality is

Ghost in the Shell features Major Motoko Kusanagi (shown here) as the central character, a female cyborg who is both smart and strong.

Ai Yazawa, whose manga series *Nana* looks at the lives of two women living together in Tokyo. Both women are named Nana, and their lives intersect by way of a chance meeting on a train. Nana Komatsu is a small-town girl who goes to Tokyo to follow her boyfriend. In contrast, Nana Osaki is a fierce punk rocker who leaves her boyfriend to pursue a musical career. More based in reality than *Ranma 1/2*, the series tackles issues of romance, careers, and women's changing roles in society. Running from 2000 to 2009, the series gained steady popularity. Two live-action movies were made in 2005 and 2006.

The widely popular *Ghost in the Shell* also features a strong female protagonist. Major Motoko Kusanagi is both intellectually and physically strong. However, there is a psychological and philosophical aspect to Motoko's character. Because Motoko is a cyborg, she causes audiences to grapple with issues of what it means to be human and how people should function and act in a world dominated by technology. This is only one of many anime and manga that address important issues avoided by Western animation for much of its history.

CHAPTER FIVE

Anime's Deeper Meaning

One of anime's more disturbing stories is *Grave of the Fireflies*. In the film, a pair of homeless orphans named Seita and Setsuko wander through a bombed Japan. From their devastated village to their life with an unbearable aunt, the story goes from bad to worse as Seita and Setsuko search for food and shelter across the devastated landscape of their country. The film features no happy ending, and in the end, after begging and stealing for food, the orphans die from starvation.

A story such as *Grave of the Fireflies* is an example of how dark anime can be. Beyond just stories of science fiction, fantasy and adventure, anime often tells moral and ethical tales that can serve as a commentary on society and culture. More specifically, because of Japan's involvement in World War II and its status as the only country to ever suffer a nuclear attack, many manga and anime works have an anti-war message.

In addition, anime and manga also confront issues such as the state of the environment or the advancement of technology and the question of whether or not humanity can adapt to such advances. As Price wrote, "Anime often disguises contemporary struggles and themes in its entertaining medium."[32]

The Japanese Experience of World War II

Anime has had a purpose other than entertainment since the days when the Japanese Imperial Navy drafted

Momotaro to help boost the morale of audiences during World War II. The war was, of course, brought to an abrupt conclusion when the United States dropped atomic bombs on the Japanese cities of Hiroshima and Nagasaki. In fact, the Allies had been bombing Japan for months before atomic weapons were unleashed on the island. In one campaign, American bombers dropped napalm canisters on several Japanese cities. Napalm is a chemical that erupts into flash fires. It was deployed in containers that resembled tin cans, which looked harmless until they struck the ground, when they exploded and burned everything near them.

One of the survivors of the napalm attacks was a teenage boy named Nosaka Akiyuki, who was living in the city of Kobe when the sky suddenly started raining napalm canisters. Akiyuki survived the attack, but his father died in the firestorm; his sister also died of starvation soon after the bombing. Akiyuki based his 1967 novel *Grave of the Fireflies* on his experiences in the Kobe firebombing. The book won the Naoki Award, which is Japan's top prize for literature, similar to the Pulitzer Prize in America. Years later, the story was produced as an anime feature film by director Isao Takahata of Studio Ghibli.

Grave of the Fireflies is a movie that promotes deep sympathy for the Japanese people, and it certainly struck a chord among Japanese audiences when it was released. However, the villains in the film are not the Americans who dropped the napalm bombs but the cold-hearted leaders of wartime Japan who led their country into war and let the two children die. Clements and McCarthy said,

> *This is an eerily quiet, sepia-toned apocalypse, accompanied by powerful subliminal messages … A crushingly sad story, beginning by revealing both characters will die, and then daring the viewer to hope they won't. Tragedy in the truest sense of the word: every moment of Takahata's masterpiece is loaded with portents of the suffering to come.*[33]

Grave of the Fireflies was released in the United States in 1993. Audiences were moved and sympathetic to the plight of the two doomed children. In 2000, when *Grave of the Fireflies* was released in a DVD version, film critic Roger Ebert said,

> *Because it is animated and from Japan,* Grave of the Fireflies *has been little seen. When anime fans say how good the film is, nobody takes them seriously. Now that it's available on DVD with a choice of subtitles or English dubbing, maybe it will find the attention it deserves. Yes, it's a cartoon … but it belongs on any list of the greatest war films ever made.*[34]

Grave of the Fireflies *is an anime film containing a deep message about war and technology.*

An Atomic Holocaust

Another anime film that portrayed the horror of a nuclear attack was 1983's *Barefoot Gen*. The film tells the story of a boy who survives the atomic blast at Hiroshima that ended World War II. In the story, Gen and his mother watch their family members burned alive by the blast, then witness their friends and neighbors slowly die from radiation poisoning.

The anime was adapted from a story that was originally published as manga. The manga artist, Keiji Nakazawa, was a survivor of Hiroshima, and his story is autobiographical. In 1966, 21 years after the atomic bomb dropped on Hiroshima, Nakazawa was living in Tokyo and working as a manga artist. That year, his mother died. She was his only close relative—his other family members died in the atomic blast. Nakazawa believed she had been afflicted with radiation poisoning as a result of the blast and that her bones withered away over the years. At that point, Nakazawa said he realized how much Japanese culture had discouraged discussion of Hiroshima and Nagasaki in any medium. To Nakazawa, it seemed as though the Japanese people learned to deal with the horrific destruction of two large cities and the deaths of more than 200,000 people simply by keeping silent about the event and pretending that it never happened. He said,

> *Since coming to Tokyo, I hadn't said a word about being an A-bomb survivor to anyone. People in Tokyo looked at you very strangely if you talked about it, so I learned to keep quiet. There was still an irrational fear among many Japanese that you could "catch" radiation sickness from A-bomb victims. There were plenty of people like that, even in a big city like Tokyo.*[35]

For that reason, Nakazawa resolved to use the medium of manga to tell the story of the atomic bomb victims. He soon produced a series, *Struck by Black Rain*, which related the story of Hiroshima survivors turning to crime to survive in postwar Japan. "*Black Rain* was published in serial form in *Manga Punch*, an adult manga magazine by a small publisher," said Nakazawa. "The big publishers turned it down. They said it was too radical for them, too political."[36]

Undisturbed by the reaction of the big publishers, Nakazawa continued to produce manga about his experiences in Hiroshima following the atomic blast. Eventually, the manga magazine *Monthly Shonen Jump* decided to publish a series of biographies of manga artists, told in manga form. Nakazawa was invited to submit his own story. He responded by producing an early version of *Barefoot Gen*, which he titled *I Saw It*. The editor of the magazine,

Keiji Nakazawa, shown here, created Barefoot Gen, *a manga that grew popular in spite of the controversy surrounding it.*

Tadasu Nagano, read the story and was awestruck by Nakazawa's experiences in Hiroshima. Nakazawa said,

> *When Nagano read it, he told me, "You should do a longer series based on this. You can make it as many pages as you want and we can run it for as long as you want." I could hardly believe it. That was the first time an editor had ever said anything like that to me. I was incredibly grateful, and felt I should do the best job*

I could. That was how Barefoot Gen *came about.*[37]

The series ran for nearly two years, until *Monthly Shonen Jump* went out of business. By then, *Barefoot Gen* had earned a following in Japan, and Nakazawa had no trouble finding another publisher willing to continue the story. In fact, *Barefoot Gen* was ultimately published in three other manga magazines. Every time one would go out of business, another magazine quickly stepped in to continue the series. In the meantime, Nakazawa found himself much in demand as a speaker before school audiences, peace groups, and similar organizations whose members were eager to hear his story of the bomb's aftermath. "At the peak, I was giving 20, 25 talks a year,"[38] he said.

Clearly, Nakazawa had been instrumental in educating a whole generation of Japanese people about the horrors of the Hiroshima bombing. The anime version of *Barefoot Gen* was released in 1983 and was followed with a sequel, *Rail of the Star*, which was produced three years later. *Rail of the Star* continued the story of Gen three years after the bombing. Since then, several other anime producers have released their own versions of the atomic attacks and how they affected the Japanese people. Two films are based on manga written by Nakazawa: *Beneath the Black Rain*, which tells the stories of three female survivors of the attack, and *Fly On, Dreamers!*, which relates the adventures of a baseball team composed of Hiroshima orphans.

Today, the anniversaries of the bombings of Hiroshima and Nagasaki are treated as national days of mourning in Japan; each city stages ceremonies to remember the victims. In addition, the Japanese media is much more comfortable with reporting news about the ceremonies and commemorative events; documentaries on Hiroshima and Nagasaki, as well as other aspects of the war, are frequently aired on Japanese TV, particularly in the days preceding the anniversary of the bombings in early August.

Still, there is no question that for years, anime and manga artists largely avoided stories that directly addressed the atomic bomb. Napier has suggested, though, that the Hiroshima and Nagasaki holocausts are a prime motivation for artists who center their science fiction stories in dismal, postapocalyptic times. Images of atomic devastation are prevalent in manga and anime, she said, even though the artists often leave it to the imagination of the viewer to figure out how the world ended up in such a mess. "The most obvious reason behind the high incidence of apocalyptic scenarios is the atomic bomb and its horrific aftereffects,"[39] she said.

The atomic bomb and the damage it inflicted is a theme that features prominently in many different anime stories. These stories often deal with the threat of nuclear war, as well as the moral and ethical dilemmas that advances in technology can create.

A Conflicted View of War

The Japanese view of war, as seen through Japanese media such as anime and manga, contains two contradictory points of view that are influenced by the country's culture and history. Author Patrick Drazen explained,

> *In its long history Japan has seen periods of nearly incessant warfare, but also hundreds of years in which the country was at peace, both at home and with its neighbors. This history contributes to Japan's current popular culture view of war: a view that is complex, if not conflicted. Wars are still fought in anime, and warriors are praised for their fighting spirit, yet a pacifist belief in the ultimate futility of war tempers these mixed messages.*
>
> *Anime depictions of war can be divided into: (a) real wars Japan was involved in, (b) fictional battles involving Japan (past, present, or future), and (c) battles with little or no connection to Earth, except that at least one of the combatant species is humanoid. The more distant the action is from any real military, the easier it is to root for one side or another without feeling like a combatant.*[1]

1. Patrick Drazen, *Anime Explosion!* Berkeley, CA: Stone Bridge Press, 2003, p. 192.

Protecting the Environment

Themes of war and atomic devastation are not the only issues tackled by Japanese anime and manga artists. Anime has a long history promoting preservation of the environment, dating back to the 1960s when *Kimba the White Lion* aired on U.S. television. The series told the story of a heroic lion cub who defended his African homeland against hunters, trappers, poachers, and other humans who aimed to destroy the animals of the jungle. In later years, anime producers continued the theme of environmental protection in such films as *Nausicaä of the Valley of Wind* and *Castle in the Sky*. Both films were produced by Miyazaki, the director of *Spirited Away*, whose environmental activism is well known in anime circles. In *Nausicaä of the Valley of the Wind*, which was produced in 1984, a young princess named Nausicaä must protect her home, the Valley of the Wind, from a sea of pollution that threatens to engulf it. The movie was based on a 1982 manga written by Miyazaki. In *Castle in the Sky*, which was made in

In Nausicaä of the Valley of the Wind, *which has a strong environmental message, Princess Nausicaä tries to study the Toxic Jungle near her home so she can understand it better.*

1986, a magical floating city known as Laputa is saved from destruction at the hands of corrupt and greedy humans. One of Miyazaki's other major works, *Princess Mononoke*, tells the story of a struggle by animals against the iron miners who threaten to wipe out their forest.

Environmental messages started making their way into anime and manga as Japan shook off the devastation of World War II and returned to a society of prosperity. The country underwent a construction boom, which meant forests and other pristine areas were leveled to make way for

new buildings. According to Toshio Suzuki, a coproducer of *Spirited Away*,

> *As we were trying to improve the economy, people worked hard to improve their living standards—but that caused much damage to our environment. Traditionally, in Japan, we were making stories about how the evil men who stole or killed would be punished by the good. We were in a social situation where the bad were destroying our environment, so it was natural for us to depict that in our films.*[40]

Even science fiction anime have included social themes, providing the stories with something more than just plots about rocket ships and heroes seeking to avenge wrongs committed by interstellar villains. Anime science fiction has questioned whether the high-tech gadgetry and environments featured in the stories are good for the human soul. A prime example of a socially conscious science fiction story is *Galaxy Express 999*, which appeared as a manga series and then was adapted into an anime series on TV in 1978. Later, the series's producers developed a feature film and sequel.

Galaxy Express 999 told of the quest of a boy named Tetsuro Hoshino (In a dubbed English version, the boy's name was changed to Joey Smith.) who sought to avenge the murder of his mother by obtaining a suit that would make him virtually indestructible. As Tetsuro and his guardian, a beautiful and mysterious woman named Maetel, search for the suit aboard an intergalactic train known as *Galaxy Express 999*, they encounter many adventures as they help the poor fend off their oppressors.

The key theme of *Galaxy Express 999*, though, is the social order that rules the universe: The very rich and powerful have given up their flesh and bones and have had their brains transferred into metal bodies, while the poor and unfortunate must stumble through life in their highly vulnerable human bodies. Therefore, each episode deals with the fundamental question of whether technology has gotten out of control—a theme that was later explored in such American movies as *The Matrix* and *The Terminator*. A final and quite subtle message about the importance of living in a low-tech world can be found in the design of *Galaxy Express 999*: As they travel from planet to planet, Tetsuro and Maetel ride in a train that resembles an old steam locomotive.

In addition to these classic anime films, more recently, as climate change and global warming have come to the forefront of social issues, Japanese artists and writers have sought to further explore the complications their country faces in the wake of such upheaval. For example, films, TV series, and games such as *Rewrite* and *Shangri-La* feature prominent environmental themes and serve as allegorical comments on nature and the need to preserve the natural world.

Rewrite is a visual novel—a type of video game where players can make

Japanese Robots

The Japanese have done more to advance the field of robot technology than any other culture. Many Japanese companies, including Sony, which is an electronics firm, as well as car manufacturers Mitsubishi and Honda, have conducted research into developing robots that are bipedal—walking on two feet—and use their eyes to see and hands to manipulate objects. Propelling this interest in biped robots is a very real social concern: With a declining population, the Japanese are concerned that in the future, there may not be enough people to perform manual labor, so they hope to develop robots to do the heavy work.

Of course, dedicated anime fans are well aware of Japan's fascination with robots, dating back to the days when *Astro Boy*, *8 Man*, and *Gigantor* hit the airwaves. Today, robots dominate Japanese anime in the *Mazinkaiser*, *Gundam*, and *RahXephon* series. British journalist John Gosling said, "It is perhaps significant that Japan is the only country in the world seriously interested in bipedal robot research, and when you look at the walking, talking, running and leaping robots of anime, you can perhaps understand why."[1]

1 John Gosling, "The Hidden World of Anime," *Animation World*, August 1996. www.awn.com/mag/issue1.5/articles/goslingcult1.5html.

This statue of Gigantor stands guard outside a train station in the city of Kobe.

choices to influence the direction of the story. It was released in 2011 and features the experiences of Kotarou Tennouji, who, though still in high school, possesses superhuman powers. With the help of five girls from his high school, he investigates unexplained mysteries of supernatural intrigue. Most of the stories in *Rewrite* take place in the fictional city of Kazamatsuri, Japan, where tree planting and afforestation have caused the city to become overgrown with trees and vegetation.

Another work that dealt with climate change was *Shangri-La*, a young adult novel that was turned into an anime series in 2009. It is set in a world where the reduction of carbon dioxide emission levels was designed to limit the global warming crises. The results are both economic and global, and in the wake of a great earthquake that hits Japan, a disparity between rich and poor occurs. The novel looks not only at current climate issues that face Japanese society but also issues of class and economic trouble.

CHAPTER SIX

A Blending of Cultures

American fans of anime become deeply embedded in Japanese tradition each time they watch an anime series on TV or watch a movie in the theater. This tradition is obvious from the moment the film or TV show starts. The visual style and soundtrack combine to create a uniquely Japanese experience.

Whether animated or live action, stories in American films are often dependent on background music. A soundtrack in an American film is frequently used to set the tone of a scene. For example, if the director wants the audience to feel sad, they might choose slow, somber music. If they want to build tension and ultimately scare the audience, they are more likely to use tones that make the audience feel uncomfortable, such as music that is not pleasant to listen to. This music generally starts low and increases in volume and tempo, or speed, as the action on the screen progresses.

Similarly, the influence of Japanese arts such as Kabuki and Noh can be seen in many anime stories. These arts are identified by basic wooden rhythm instruments, which are used to create a feeling of suspense among the audience. In addition to musical instruments, other sounds are often used to set tones and moods. For example, anime creators may use the sound of an insect called a semi, known as a cicada in English, to help set the atmosphere. Since cicadas are heard only on the hottest days, the audience will understand that the scene they are watching is taking place in intense heat. In the series *Neon Genesis Evangelion*, an anime about a futuristic version of Tokyo set in a world that has suffered intense climate change after an apocalyptic event, cicadas are heard throughout the show to remind viewers that the world is much hotter than normal.

These unique details have helped to strengthen anime's tradition. Censorship and localization issues still exist, but it is far easier to access unchanged anime and manga than it previously was. The style has come a long way since the attempts to westernize *Astro Boy* with choppy editing. Instead, the story that Japanese artists and writers tell is the story that American audiences now watch on their TV screens. Characters in anime are distinctly Japanese: They often wear kimonos, dine with chopsticks, and pray to Buddha. This loyalty to tradition has maintained the artistic characteristics of the genre while also exposing American audiences to Japanese culture.

Many anime and manga are influenced by Kabuki and Noh theater, and some show characters wearing traditional Japanese clothing.

Reflecting Old Tradition

The influences of the ancient Japanese theater arts of Kabuki and Noh on anime do not stop with the background music. Even the artistic style of the animators reflects many of the old traditions. According to John Gosling,

> *Just watch an anime character giving a speech or monologue and you will often see that the whole body is used to express his or her sentiments. The character assumes a series of stylized and exaggerated postures, which in spirit echoes the philosophy of the kabuki actor, who from an early age is trained in dance and other techniques to use the entire body as a medium of expression.*[41]

Indeed, Gosling suggested that anyone familiar with Kabuki theater can see Kabuki movements in anime. For example, most animators open their films and TV episodes with still portraits of their characters—particularly

Long-Standing Tradition

The theatrical genres known as Noh and Kabuki have inspired many anime artists. Both forms of theater feature elaborately decorated costumes and rituals that have remained unchanged since actors first took the stage centuries ago.

In Noh, which was first performed in the 14th century, the dramas typically portray the stories of gods, spirits, or great warriors from Japan's history. Noh actors wear patterned costumes and masks and perform under roofed stages. One of the traditions of Noh requires the performers to rehearse separately under the guidance of a teacher. The actors never take the stage together until they are in front of an audience, which means they sometimes have to think quickly during the performance.

Kabuki dates back to the 17th century and was originally a form of dance performed by female entertainers. The government considered the dancing too provocative, so it banned women from performing in 1629. From that time on, Kabuki theater has been a male-dominated art form; men even play the female roles. As in Noh, Kabuki actors perform in ornate costumes, but they wear makeup instead of masks. Most Kabuki stories relate famous acts of heroism or sacrifice in Japanese history. Unlike most plays, which may run for two or three hours, Kabuki performances can go on all day. Theatergoers often do not sit through the whole play but take a few hours from their day to sit in on part of the performance.

In Kabuki theater, men play all the parts, even when the character is a woman. Many people believe the poses of Kabuki actors have influenced the way anime artists draw their characters.

in anime that feature ensemble casts with many characters. Clearly, Gosling said, the poses struck by the characters in the introductory still frames are modeled after the *mie* and *kimari* poses—the most dramatic moments in Kabuki theater when the character draws a sword or clutches a fan and stands rock-still so that the audience can soak in the meaning of the moment. (*Mie* poses are struck by male characters; *kimari* poses are assumed by females.)

Meanwhile, in Noh theater, it is common for characters to huddle together on the side of the stage and perform a little skit that has nothing to do with the main story that is unfolding on center stage. Gosling said that is a common technique used in anime as well, generally added to the stories for comic relief purposes. He believes Japanese animators may have gotten the idea for these little comedic asides from productions of Noh theater.

Subtle Messages

Some examples of Japanese culture found in anime and manga are far more subtle than the Kabuki poses and Noh skits, and people generally have to be familiar with Japanese culture to recognize them. Still, they are depicted on the screen or in the pages of manga, and through some careful observation, they can be recognized.

One example is cherry blossoms, which have a special meaning in Japan—they bloom in spring, but they also foretell death. Price said, "The cherry blossom only blooms for about three days out of the year. It is this impermanence that makes it so highly regarded and symbolic in Japanese culture."[42] For this reason, when a character dies in anime or manga, cherry blossoms are sometimes seen nearby. The body may be buried under a cherry tree or the artist may show cherry blossom petals falling when people speak about the character.

Some of the symbols used to communicate emotion or specific actions are also unique to Japan and may be confusing to Western viewers the first time they encounter them. Some of these include:

- *Scratching the back of the head when embarrassed*
- *The appearance of a giant drop of sweat (not to be mistaken for a teardrop) or the apparent outline of a large X on a character's temple in times of stress …*
- *A large bubble of phlegm coming from a character's nose denoting that the character is asleep.*[43]

A drop of sweat or the outline of what looks like an X indicates emotion. Depending on the situation, it may show that the character is stressed, embarrassed, or angry.

Breaking the Rules of Myth

Another way Kabuki's influence can be seen in anime is that the lines between good and evil—right and wrong—are often less clear-cut than in Western works. Many Western stories follow a pattern, or template, called the hero's journey. This story template was established by the ancient Greeks and is still used today by many writers and filmmakers. Two examples of the hero's journey template are *The Lord of the Rings* and *The Wizard of Oz*.

An Education in Manga

Manga and anime have grown into a $5 billion-a-year industry in Japan, but until recently, most artists were self-taught or graduates of general art programs at Japanese universities. In 2000, though, Kyoto Seika University in the city of Kyoto established a manga program. In 2006, the program announced its first group of full-time faculty. In addition, the university has established the Kyoto International Manga Museum. In 2011, the university announced the establishment of Japan's first ever manga doctoral program.

Keiichi Makino, the former head of the university's manga program, said the program has helped legitimize the profession, which has often been held in low esteem by college professors as well as other Japanese artists. In the brief time the school has offered the program, Makino said, it has clearly helped some manga artists get their start. "We went out on a limb," he said. "We had doubts about the viability of teaching in a university setting, especially since a lot of academics considered manga 'trashy.'"[1]

Kyoto Seika University established the Kyoto International Manga Museum, which is shown here.

1. Quoted in "Mad About Manga," *Chronicle of Higher Education*, July 28, 2006, p. A-31.

These are two vastly different stories, yet they follow the same familiar pattern. The stories begin with the introduction of the hero or heroine and the call to adventure. Next, the reader is introduced to a character who is wiser and serves as a mentor. In *The Lord of the Rings*, the wizard Gandalf advises Frodo the Hobbit; in *The Wizard of Oz*, Glinda the good witch guides Dorothy. Next, the hero begins a journey and along the way enlists friends and allies to go along to provide help (Aragorn, Legolas, and Gimli in *The Lord of the Rings*; the Lion, Scarecrow, and Tin Woodsman in *The Wizard of Oz*). There are many tests and ordeals along the way, which the central characters endure and overcome. The hero or heroine may even suffer through a period of self-doubt, but in the end, he or she resolves to go on. Finally, the journey ends with a confrontation against the villain. In *The Lord of the Rings*, Sauron is defeated, and Frodo destroys the ring; in *The Wizard of Oz*, Dorothy captures the broom from the Wicked Witch of the West, melts her with a bucket of water, and uses the ruby slippers to return to Kansas.

However, anime and manga often do not follow this pattern. In Japanese storytelling, the hero may have a dark side. Sometimes the hero may not survive the story—he or she will be killed off before the end. The villain may be misunderstood. When the villain dies, he or she may gain sympathy from the audience. According to Price, the Japanese have adapted the fantastic and mythological stories of manga and anime from life in the real world. In the real world, the good guys do not always win, and the bad guys may not always be so bad after all.

In *Princess Mononoke*, there is no question that Mononoke is the heroine and Lady Eboshi the villain. However, Mononoke is often portrayed as a cold-blooded huntress, while Lady Eboshi emerges as a sympathetic character. In the inevitable final battle, Lady Eboshi loses an arm but survives and returns to Irontown, committed to building a new community that will respect the forest life. In another anime, *Death Note*, the main character, Light Yagami, finds a notebook that kills anyone whose name is written in it. He uses the notebook to kill criminals; he feels he is doing the right thing, but the police disagree and try to stop him. The series explores the ideas of good and evil, and the viewers must decide for themselves whether Light is a good or bad character.

In the mythology portrayed in anime and manga, one trend becomes very clear: Japanese mythology is not very mythological after all. Whether Americans know it or not when they see these stories unfold before their eyes, they are seeing mythology told from a uniquely Japanese point of view. Price said,

The characters in *Cowboy Bebop* (shown here) are bounty hunters—people hired by the police to catch criminals. However, they are not perfectly good; one is a former criminal, one is a hacker, and one is a thief.

> *Perhaps the most intriguing aspect of Japanese animation to American viewers is its realistic approach to mature, relatable topics and its sincere depiction of human emotion. Fans often comment on how anime's creative storylines are treated with genuine, non-glossed over honesty. Characters don't live happily ever after, bad things happen to good people, and villains go unpunished. The Japanese aesthetic tradition of … art just so happens to mirror real life situations.*[44]

The Spirit World

Religion and spirits play a large part in many anime and manga. For instance, in *Princess Mononoke*, the gods of the forest are important characters, and in *Spirited Away*, Chihiro stays for several weeks at a bathhouse for spirits. Sometimes, the spirit characters are friendly; other times, they are terrifying. Anime features some uniquely Japanese spirits, as well as mythological creatures from Western tales. Drazen described the role of the supernatural in an anime called *Vampire Princess Miyu*, which he considers a must-see. In the show, exorcist Himiko Se crosses paths with Miyu, a vampire who will forever remain 14 years old:

> *Himiko also learns of an order of being that's part demon, part human, called a Shinma, who must be returned to the Underworld by Miyu and her companion Larva. With or without Miyu's help, HImiko has to deal with a vampire, a possessed suit of armor, and an enchantress who turns people into marionettes. In the final installment, she confronts Miyu directly and learns her story.*[1]

In **My Neighbor Totoro**, *a little girl befriends a forest spirit named Totoro.*

1. Patrick Drazen, *Anime Explosion!* Berkeley, CA: Stone Bridge Press, 2003, p. 161.

Dedicated Fans

In the United States, anime and manga have achieved widespread popularity. Both commercially and culturally, Japanese animation has reached incredible heights. Although anime and manga are far more widely watched and read in Japan than they are in the United States, they have a dedicated American fan base that includes people of all ages.

Anime fans admire the talent of the artists as well as the writers. The style of drawing is different than in the West, but that does not make it any less impressive. Western animators have occasionally been influenced by the drawing style and the themes in the stories, just as Japanese animators were originally influenced by Disney. However, these influences have not overpowered the uniquely Japanese point of view that can be seen in most works of anime and manga. Through these works, Western fans can learn more about Japanese culture while enjoying a wide range of beautifully drawn stories.

Introduction: Anime: A Global Phenomenon

1. Shinobu Price, "Cartoons from Another Planet: Japanese Animation as Cross-Cultural Communication," *Journal of American and Comparative Cultures*, Spring 2001, p. 153.
2. Nissim Otmazgin, "Anime in the US: The Entrepreneurial Dimensions of Globalized Culture," *Pacific Affairs*, vol. 87, no. 1, March 2014, p. 53.

Chapter One: Anime's Origins

3. Quoted in Henry (Yoshitaka) Kiyama and Frederik L. Schodt, *The Four Immigrants Manga: A Japanese Experience in San Francisco, 1904–1924*. Berkeley, CA: Stone Bridge, 2005, pp. 7–8.
4. Quoted in "Japan Finds Films by Early 'Anime' Pioneers," Reuters, March 27, 2008. www.reuters.com/article/us-japan-anime-pioneers-idUST23069120080327.
5. Gilles Poitras, *Anime Essentials*. Berkeley, CA: Stone Bridge, 2005, pp. 16–17.
6. Quoted in "Interview with Mr. Frederik Schodt: Writer and Manga Scholar," *Japan Foundation Newsletter*, June/July 2005, pp. 1–2.
7. Fred Patten, *Watching Anime, Reading Manga: 25 Years of Essays and Reviews*. Berkeley, CA: Stone Bridge, 2004, p. 271.

Chapter Two: Americanizing Anime

8. Patten, *Watching Anime, Reading Manga*, p. 129.

9. Quoted in Harvey Deneroff, "Fred Ladd: An Interview," *Animation World*, August 1996. www.awn.com/mag/issue1.5/articles/deneroffladd1.5.html.
10. Jonathan Clements and Helen McCarthy, *The Anime Encyclopedia*. Berkeley, CA: Stone Bridge, 2001, p. 374.
11. Patten, *Watching Anime, Reading Manga*, p. 59.
12. Quoted in Patten, *Watching Anime, Reading Manga*, p. 306.
13. Clements and McCarthy, *The Anime Encyclopedia*, p. 9.
14. Janet Maslin, "A Tokyo of the Future in Vibrant Animation," *New York Times*, October 19, 1990, p. C-12.
15. Roger Ebert, "*Spirited Away*," *Chicago Sun-Times*, September 20, 2002. rogerebert.suntimes.com/apps/pbcs.dll/article?AID=/20020920/REVIEWS/209200306/1023.
16. Nicolas Rapold, "Life, a Royal Pain," *New York Times*, October 16, 2014. www.nytimes.com/2014/10/17/movies/the-tale-of-the-princess-kaguya-from-isao-takahata.html?_r=0.

Chapter Three: Why Anime Stands Out

17. Christopher Hart, *Anime Mania: How to Draw Characters for Japanese Animation*. New York, NY: Watson-Guptill, 2002, p. 7.
18. Latonya Pennington, "Why Anime Characters Aren't Meant to Be White," *Revelist*, April 18, 2016. www.revelist.com/real-talk/stop-whitewashing-asian-characters/1672.
19. Poitras, *Anime Essentials*, p. 62.
20. Hart, *Anime Mania*, p. 22.
21. Poitras, *Anime Essentials*, p. 58.
22. Rachel Cantrell, "Manga and its Impact on the Graphic Novel," in *History, Theme, and Technique*, ed. Bart H. Beaty and Stephen Weiner. Ipswich, MA: Salem Press, 2013, p. 195.

Chapter Four: Anime's Strong Female Roles

23. Price, "Cartoons from Another Planet," p. 157.
24. Quoted in George Gene Gustines, "For Graphic Novels, a New Frontier: Teenage Girls," *New York Times*, November 25, 2006, p. B-7.

25. Alexis Brazier, "Hypersexualization of Women in Anime Is Not Okay," *Technique*, October 2, 2015. nique.net/opinions/2015/10/02/hypersexualization-of-women-in-anime-is-not-okay/.
26. Brazier, "Hypersexualization of Women in Anime Is Not Okay."
27. Quoted in Caitlin White, "Women in Comics, Graphic Novels Finally Getting the Spotlight They Have Deserved for Generations," Bustle, January 16, 2015. www.bustle.com/articles/58807-women-in-comics-graphic-novels-finally-getting-the-spotlight-they-have-deserved-for-generations.
28. Poitras, *Anime Essentials*, p. 44.
29. Quoted in Charles Solomon, "Four Mothers of Manga Gain American Fans with Expertise in a Variety of Visual Styles," *New York Times*, November 28, 2006, p. E-5.
30. Rachel Cantrell, "Cardcaptor Sakura," in *Manga (Critical Survey of Graphic Novels)*, eds. Bart H. Beaty and Stephen Weiner. Ipswich, MA: Salem Press, 2012, p. 72.
31. Susan J. Napier, *Anime: From Akira to Princess Mononoke*. New York: Palgrave, 2000, p. 55.

Chapter Five: Anime's Deeper Meaning

32. Price, "Cartoons from Another Planet," p. 153.
33. Clements and McCarthy, *The Anime Encyclopedia*, pp. 153–154.
34. Roger Ebert, "*Grave of the Fireflies*," *Chicago Sun-Times*, March 19, 2000. rogerebert.suntimes.com/apps/pbcs.dll/article?AID=/20000319/REVIEWS08/3190301/1023.
35. Quoted in Alan Gleason, "Keiji Nakazawa," *Comics Journal*, no. 256. www.tcj.com/256/i_nakazawa.html.
36. Quoted in Gleason, "Keiji Nakazawa."
37. Quoted in Gleason, "Keiji Nakazawa."
38. Quoted in Gleason, "Keiji Nakazawa."
39. Napier, *Anime: From Akira to Princess Mononoke*, p. 29.
40. Quoted in Lynden Barber, "Anime at the Gates," *Australian*, May 15, 2004.

Chapter Six: A Blending of Cultures

41. Gosling, "The Hidden World of Anime."
42. Price, "Cartoons from Another Planet," p. 153.
43. Patrick Drazen, *Anime Explosion!* Berkeley, CA: Stone Bridge Press, 2003, p. 25.
44. Price, "Cartoons from Another Planet," p. 153.

For More Information

Books

Ban, Toshia. *The Osamu Tezuka Story: A Life in Manga and Anime*. Berkeley, CA: Stone Bridge Press, 2016.

This graphic format biography discusses the artist's immense influence on anime and manga.

Baricordi, Andrea, et. al. *Anime: A Guide to Japanese Animation (1958–1988)*. Quebec, Canada: Protoculture Inc., 2000.

This book is an essential reference that spans more than 30 years of classic anime.

Bendazzi, Giannalberto. *Animation: A World History: Volume II: The Birth of a Style—The Three Markets*. Boca Raton, FLA: CRC Press, 2016.

This book views and discusses animation with a scholarly voice. It covers the importance of anime and its place in the history of animation.

Clements, Jonathan, and Helen McCarthy. *The Anime Encyclopedia: A Century of Japanese Animation (3rd Revised Edition)*. Berkeley, CA: Stone Bridge Press, 2015.

This comprehensive overview of anime gives a history of the craft since 1917 and features capsule reviews of virtually every animated film produced in Japan since then.

Denison, Ray. *Anime: A Critical Introduction*. London, UK: Bloomsbury Academic Publishing, 2015.

This book features commentary on different styles and forms of anime throughout the years.

Hart, Christopher. *Anime Mania: How to Draw Characters for Japanese Animation*. New York, NY: Watson-Guptill, 2002.

Hart, an American cartoonist and art teacher, walks students through the entire process of drawing anime characters—from preliminary pencil sketches to completing the elaborate and colorful portraits of the characters.

Websites

Anime News Network

www.animenewsnetwork.com

Anime News Network is the leading English-language news source for all things anime, manga, video games, and Japanese pop culture.

Anime Planet

www.anime-planet.com/anime/all

Anime Planet features a database of the most popular anime films and TV shows. This website contains more than 40,000 legal streaming episodes and allows viewers to create lists of previously viewed material. Ask a parent or guardian before buying a subscription.

Crunchyroll

www.crunchyroll.com/videos/anime

The Internet's leading anime streaming service, Crunchyroll features a back catalogue of anime series, as well as new series available when they air in Japan. It is a great place to view anime films and TV shows. Ask a parent or guardian before buying a subscription.

IMDb
www.imdb.com

This website contains information about many anime works, including summaries, voice actors, photos, quotes, trivia, and more.

Nerdist: "The Best Anime for Beginners to Watch"
nerdist.com/the-best-anime-for-beginners-to-watch/

Nerdist is a website that posts news and reviews about games, movies, and comics. This article lists the author's picks for the 10 best anime for beginners.

That Anime Project
www.umich.edu/~anime/index.html

Created by the University of Michigan Japanese Animation Group, this website provides an introduction to anime for those who are unfamiliar with the genre.

Index

F

G

H

J

K

L

M

T

V

W

X

Y

Picture Credits

Cover portishead1/E+/Getty Images; pp. 1, 3–4, 6, 13, 25, 41, 56, 68, 81, 92, 96, 99, 103, 104 (title background) Lunarus/Shutterstock.com; p. 7 tulpahn/ Shutterstock.com; p. 9 Photograph By David Messent/Photolibrary/Getty Images; p. 11 (main) 360b/Shutterstock.com; pp. 11 (inset), 23 neftali/ Shutterstock.com; pp. 14, 21, 26, 38, 47, 51, 55, 57, 59, 66, 79 (caption background) Jaroslav Machacek/Shutterstock.com; p. 14 DEA/G. DAGLI ORTI/De Agostini Picture Library/Getty Images; p. 16 Liza Ievleva/ Shutterstock.com; p. 18 Sasuke88/Wikimedia Commons; pp. 20–21 (top) spatuletail/Shutterstock.com; pp. 20–21 (bottom) beeboys/ Shutterstock.com; p. 26 VCG/VCG via Getty Images; p. 29 United Archives GmbH/Alamy Stock Photo; p. 32 Sinisha Karich/Shutterstock.com; p. 37 Moviestore collection Ltd/Alamy Stock Photo; p. 38 Entertainment Pictures/ Alamy Stock Photo; p. 39 Frazer Harrison/Getty Images; p. 41 © istockphoto.com/deedl; pp. 42, 57, 90 Photo 12/Alamy Stock Photo; p. 44 anpannan/Shutterstock.com; p. 47 Imagine Photographer/ Shutterstock.com; pp. 48–49 Frank Carter/Lonely Planet Images/ Shutterstock.com; p. 51 YOSHIKAZU TSUNO/AFP/Getty Images; p. 53 BRENDAN SMIALOWSKI/AFP/Getty Images; pp. 54–55 Phillip Maguire/ Shutterstock.com; p. 59 Videowokart/Shutterstock.com; p. 62 Liron Peer/ Shutterstock.com; p. 66 Ronald Grant Archive/Alamy Stock Photo; p. 70 STUDIO GHIBLI/Ronald Grant Archive/Alamy Stock Photo; p. 72 JIJI PRESS/AFP/Getty Images; p. 74 Courtesy of the Library of Congress; pp. 76–77, 89 AF archive/Alamy Stock Photo; p. 79 © istockphoto.com/ SeanPavonePhoto; p. 82 maxwindy/Shutterstock.com; p. 84 Koichi Kamoshida/Getty Images; p. 86 Juan David Giraldo/Shutterstock.com; p. 87 cowardlion/Shutterstock.com; back cover vector illustration/ Shutterstock.com.

About the Author

Kenneth Bartolotta is a college writing teacher and former journalist. In his spare time, he is a textbook editor and fiction writer. He lives in Buffalo, New York.